VICKY

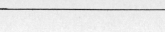

VICKY

A BRIDGE BETWEEN TWO WORLDS

Ursula Burton

DARTON, LONGMAN AND TODD
LONDON

First published in 1991 by
Darton, Longman and Todd Ltd
89 Lillie Road, London SW6 1UD

ISBN 0–232–51956–0

A catalogue record for this book is available
from the British Library

Phototypeset in 12/13½pt Garamond by Intype, London
Printed and bound in Great Britain by
Courier International, East Kilbride

CONTENTS

We must think of those who have died as alive and joyful . . . our life only separated from theirs by the thinnest of veils.

Abbé de Tourville

FOREWORD

Victoria Maclay was a vibrant person, a young wife and mother who died tragically after an anaesthetic disaster in the course of a routine gynaecological operation. Her death, however, was far from being instantaneous, for although the higher rational, communicating centres of her brain were demolished, the basic vegetative areas of immediate survival, such as circulation and breathing, remained intact. And so Victoria survived in her damaged body for nearly two years.

Her survival, however, was not that of a human vegetable that we so often read about in connection with senile degeneration of the brain. Although she could not communicate in any tangible way, there remained a glow about her which convinced many who visited her that she was still aware in a superconscious state; certainly many of her visitors felt uplifted by her presence as she lay quietly in her bed. When she eventually died, there was a sense of a soul leaving for a new assignation. During the ensuing months a number of people were aware of her loving presence around them for short periods of time. The accounts of these personal experiences form the bulk of this book, which is to be welcomed as a source of consolation for many other bereaved people. Indeed there is more than mere consolation in these accounts; there is a conviction of the survival of the essential part of Victoria's personality which is proceeding to a full encounter with God for work ahead. Of these matters we can speak only tentatively, but it should be noted that the help of mediums was not invoked to contact Vicky's soul. On the contrary it was she who initiated contact in order to reassure others of her continued survival. I believe that this sort of postmortem communication will become even more common in the future as people become more sensitive to other realms of existence as a prelude to their own death, transition, and growth in the world beyond physical dissolution.

MARTIN ISRAEL

INTRODUCTION

In the autumn of 1982, the Jesuit Spirituality Centre at St Beuno's, North Wales, began the first of its three-month residential courses. The course, open to all Christian denominations, was originally designed for lay men and women, as well as for Religious and clergy, who were already engaged, or were about to engage, in the work of spiritual direction and retreat-giving. The core of the course was a period of thirty days, during which participants would make the full Spiritual Exercises of St Ignatius Loyola.

Shortly before the first three-month course was due to begin, the one laywoman who had applied wrote asking if she might attend the first half of the course only, which included the thirty-day retreat, postponing attendance at the second half until the following year. The reason for her request was, she explained, that she had developed cancer, and her consultant was advising immediate surgery. Having already undergone surgery for cancer, she was unwilling to have any more and believed that there were other ways of dealing with the illness. However, she thought it would be wiser to postpone the second half of the course until the following year when her health would have improved!

She came and made the full Spiritual Exercises, which I gave to her. I expected that her attention would be focused on her illness and the possibility that it might be terminal. During the thirty days, when I met with her daily, she never, as far as I remember, spoke of her illness. Her silence, as I soon realized, was not because she could not face the reality of her condition, but because she did not consider her cancer to be a question of major importance, nor death to be a tragedy.

After the retreat, she returned home to face more medical tests. The consultant was amazed: the tumour had diminished and soon disappeared entirely. The following year she returned to St Beuno's to complete the second part of the course, and for many years afterwards she returned as a member of the retreat-giving staff.

The laywoman is Ursula Burton, author of this book. A few years after her own cancer, she had to face a tragedy which, for her, was far more painful to bear: the anaesthetic accident which left her daughter, Vicky, mother of three young children, living but helpless, immobile and incapable of communicating in any tangible way. I visited the hospital on one occasion with Angus, Vicky's husband, and Ursula, and for a few minutes felt something of the dark desolation and grief which was to afflict them for almost two years.

There are many different ways of coping with the pain of loss. The most common is by way of escape, and there are many different routes. We can anaesthetize ourselves against the pain of reality by drugs or drink, or by retreating into a fantasy world, where the person or situation we have lost becomes for us the only living reality, or we can immerse ourselves in activity, refusing to face the reality of our loss by blocking out the painful memories. This latter method can be just as damaging as the way of drugs or fantasy, but is often commended by a society itself unable to cope with death, and praised as 'brave', 'courageous', 'behaving normally'.

After reading this book the reader will begin to understand why, in her thirty-day retreat, Ursula did not consider her cancer to be of primary importance, nor death to be a tragedy. The same attitude is now expressed in the way she struggles with her grief at her daughter's affliction and death. She does not ignore the tragedy, nor try to escape from the reality and pain of it: she acknowledges it, faces the horror of it, embraces it, yields to it, and in so doing she discovers new meaning not only in her own pain and grief, but in life itself, and in death.

Our conscious minds grasp only a tiny fraction of the reality in which we live. Much of the pain and frustration we suffer is because we assume that what we consciously perceive is the total reality, so death seems the end, the final tragedy. *Vicky – A Bridge Between Two Worlds* questions our unquestioned assumptions, releasing the mind from its self-imprisonment, and giving us a glimpse of the miracle in which we are now living, and in which we shall continue to live after death. The book's starting point is a private grief, but it leads the reader to a new perspective on life and death and one begins to understand why the author did not look on her own cancer as of primary importance, nor the prospect of death as tragic.

GERARD W. HUGHES

PROLOGUE

In May 1984 my eldest daughter, 34 years old and happily married mother of three children, received brain damage, due to lack of oxygen while under an anaesthetic for a minor operation, resulting in her death two years later.

The first few weeks after the accident we were all numbed by shock. It was as if an invisible machine kept me going as I went about the usual chores, automatically reacting to events. Through it all I was aware of being upheld and given strength to carry on through the support of those who had already gone on, as well as from the love and thoughts of friends, both near and far.

From the start we were told that the damage to the brain had been severe, especially to the left hemisphere. Repeatedly the doctors would tell us that there was very little hope of any significant recovery; repeatedly it failed to register in my mind. Others would tell us that we must hope, for while there is life there is hope; and miracles still happen. Hope kept returning. I found this created an ambivalent attitude which was very draining. Maybe hope is part of our emotional survival kit but for me it would have been more helpful and comforting to have been reassured that 'All life is moving towards this new beginning, and that it is but a transition into

3

a gloriously liberated life'. I began to wonder if people really did believe that we are anything more than this physical body? Perhaps they are not really sure that there is another existence on a different level?

In order to try and re-activate Vicky's brain cells, various approaches were tried, orthodox and unorthodox, which made me realize how little the medical profession knows about the function of the brain. Vicky was given homoeopathic remedies to help restore her to a more peaceful state when she became distressed, and they did alleviate any agitation. My gratitude to the hospital staff who co-operated so willingly in the giving of these powders is beyond words. Although the powders were not easy to ingest as Vicky had no conscious swallowing reaction, we knew it would have been her wish to be given homoeopathic treatment as she used it for herself and her family, and so both her wishes and ours were sensitively honoured.

During Vicky's two years in her hospital bed she made herself felt to other people in other places. I write hesitantly and tentatively about the times I felt her presence after her death, as I have been brought up to label such experiences as belonging to the paranormal and therefore suspect; certainly experiences quickly to be dismissed. All I can say is that at the time they felt more real than reality, and that when one has experienced this other dimension one knows, without a shadow of doubt, that it contains, and is, the deeper reality. It is different, but within that difference a call is heard asking for recognition.

None of us ever sought the experience; always it came at unexpected moments. It is not easy to explain what I felt. I can only liken the energies that passed through my body to those of an electric shock. There

4

was no doubt in my mind that it was Vicky. At first the current was very powerful, but later on less so. Maybe the energies from this other dimension need to be lowered, in the same way as voltage can be lowered, if interaction with our present vibrations is to take place.

We must not be fearful or resistant but receive what can be comfortably absorbed. Those who have passed on have to be patient and learn to adjust their power, so that eventually this osmosis and intermingling of energies can be used for the good of the whole. The veil between the two worlds is becoming thinner for a purpose and Revelation 21:1–4 may have something to say to us:

> I saw a new heaven and a new earth, the first heaven, and the first earth had disappeared now, and there was no longer any sea. I saw the holy city and the New Jerusalem, coming down from God out of heaven, made ready like a bride adorned for her husband. I heard a loud voice proclaiming from the throne: 'Now at last God has his dwelling among men. He will dwell among them and they shall be his people, and God himself will be with them. He will wipe every tear from their eyes; there shall be an end to death, and to mourning and crying and pain; for the old order has passed away.'

I believe that the various signs and nudges I and others have received from Vicky are for the purpose of awakening us to the reality of other dimensions; to show us that we are members one with another, interdependent and interconnected, living in one space. All of us are called to be co-creators in building the Kingdom, the New World, thus helping the evolution of the planet.

Those who have gone before us, the Communion of

Saints, the Elder Brethren, can see with a wider vision, and must want to help us break out of our conditioned, linear thinking, to enable us to build a better world, and save this planet from self-destruction.

A concerted effort to save humanity from itself is required, and we have to learn how to communicate with, respond to, and receive those finer energies. These souls initiate a connection with us when there is a reason to do so, and when we are receptive. They 'up there' need our co-operation, and we 'down here' need their help in this rescue operation. The task is now so big that it calls for the action of all souls, whether incarnate or discarnate.

Christopher Fry wrote:

> Thank God our time is now when wrong
> Comes up to face us everywhere,
> Never to leave us till we take
> The longest stride of soul men ever took.
> Affairs are now soul size.
> The enterprise
> Is exploration into God.
> Where are you making for? It takes
> So many thousand years to wake,
> But will you wake for pity's sake?

My reason for telling the story is twofold. I believe that this would have been Vicky's wish if we could have discussed it before the accident, as we shared thoughts which went beyond traditional, orthodox beliefs, and I do not doubt that from where she is at this time she would like this area of communication opened up. Secondly, I believe we are all approaching a transition of consciousness which can be seen to be moving rapidly, affecting and disturbing our familiar structures of society, be they in medicine, education, ecology or religion. Our highly technical and rational approach, which is the function of the left hemisphere of the brain, has reached a point where we are in danger of destroying ourselves and our world, unless we can cultivate the right hemisphere, the intuitive, creative, aspect, in order to redress the purely intellectual way of operating. We have forgotten that feelings and intuition may often be wiser than the mind. Is it incidental that it was Vicky's left hemisphere of the brain that was damaged?

The bringing together of the two halves of the brain, and allowing the unconscious to fuse into the conscious, is part of the integration of the person which must occur before we can become whole, undivided people – fully alive, imbued with God-consciousness as opposed to self-consciousness. We all have to move from the sense of being a monad, of being a soul in isolation, to the sense of being part of the greater living whole.

'The old order has passed away' and we are called to move on to new pastures, to the new age, for we cannot cling to the past with its outworn thought patterns and still survive in a world that is ever evolving.

This is a book about a subject that no one likes to dwell on today: death. It was whilst living through the two years of my daughter's hospitalization that I came to this deeper realization that we are more than our physical body; indeed more than our brain. I had known this intellectually but I had not experienced the truth it encapsulated.

The real, immortal part of us – our unique essence or personality – cannot be destroyed, no matter what violence is done to our physical body. Death is but a birth into a less restricted form of life; the transition being akin to the chrysalis that turns into the butterfly. Nevertheless it is very hard to accept personal loss and to know God's ways are wiser than ours can ever be.

I found my focus was on losing a daughter and what that would mean to her husband and young family. So, in spite of believing that when we pass on to our next phase we inhabit a space that frees us from earthly limitations, the pain and fear of loss was not lessened. The emotions attached to my personal grief were overwhelming and obscured that perception. Fear can be a most destructive emotion and needs to be recognized for the blinding and paralysing effect it can have on us. It can creep in when any form of change takes place, and we need to look at our resistance and endeavour to see beyond the outer appearance. We will find that within the traumas and suffering of this world lies a lesson. I learnt that we have to live with the facts of life, the good and the not-so-good, and accept them, take them by the hand and walk with the tension they create. In time, this acceptance transforms the positive and negative aspects, gathers them up to a point that is beyond 'goodness' and 'badness' as we see it, and takes them into the Whole: God, which is greater than either.

I have experienced the trauma of divorce, undergone major surgery for cancer three times and suffered bereavement, but is there anyone who has not been through some form of extreme upheaval in recent years? Relationships that seemed to be made for eternity crumble in the most bizarre ways. Nothing is permanent any more: the things of this world are revealed as transitory and bring no sense of security. This disintegration is not only at a personal level. It is reflected at a national level, in politics and business. There is very little trust left. On the international scene the power and greed that is rife could cause the monetary system of the world to collapse; and abuse of the environment and escalating pollution herald further geographical disasters that could reduce future life on our planet to a very different form.

But this book is also about hope: the hope that lies beyond the pain and suffering that we go through in their many forms. Suffering gives us the opportunity to change. Change is constant and everything is in flux, as Heraclitus said nearly 3,000 years ago; but the pace of change in the twentieth century has become like a roaring torrent.

When our thinking changes we shall be released from our blinkered vision and a new world will be revealed which as yet we scarcely know, or are afraid to look at. This new world is one in which we can discover that we are all part of the One, that there is no separation and that God is closer to us than we are to ourselves. In the words of St Catherine of Genoa, 'My God is me; nor do I recognize any other me, except my God himself'. We can never be alone for all creation is a unity, and death is but a bridge to that other dimension of which we have already had a glimpse.

I believe that with the recognition that all life is contained within the cosmic space which we call the universe, we shall be able to move more easily from one dimension to another, and thus serve and help each other in new and wider ways. This story portrays an aspect of Vicky's nature and thinking which she and I were just beginning to share and explore together, and for me this communication feels like a continuation of the exchange. She was essentially a wife and mother with little time for 'other-worldly' matters; her main concern was for her husband and children and the home they had made together. I have no doubt that this is her concern today, and that she is still very much a part of her family and involved in their well-being.

Vicky has helped me to see, as others have before her, that the veil between the worlds is thin. The Bridge is there if we have the courage to use it and to let go of our limited perspective which more often belongs to the realm of illusion than of reality.

The letters which follow are from part of a series written by myself and others to Mrs Dorothy Ivens, a lifelong friend of both Vicky and myself. She is a lady of great wisdom and charity, who although old in years, being now in her 103rd year, is ageless because her spirit is free and unfettered. On retirement, she and her husband Ralph gave up their home in Kent and bought and converted an ancient Thames fire boat in which they sailed up the east coast of Scotland, finally mooring on the shores of Loch Ness. Here they lived a simple, quiet and inwardly rich life, which they shared with those who went aboard their boat. Ralph was renowned for his home-baked bread which was put to rise in the sun, in the wheelhouse. One slice of that and you were set up for the day. But it was the spiritual sustenance they offered that drew people from far and wide. Ralph coached those who sought him out in languages and philosophy, while Dorothy got on with writing her books. Their lives were lived to the full.

In the second part of the book, I reflect on the experience of Vicky's accident and all that followed, and see it nudging me to new ways of perceiving and understanding life, death and God; and that the Spirit does indeed hover over the chaos.

LETTERS

My dear,

At last there is a little space in which to put pen to paper. Where does time go these days? Is it our imagination that it has speeded up, it can hardly be due to our advancing years as all age groups seem to be aware of an 'acceleration' of the days, weeks and months.

As I go about my chores, my mind is chatting to you, but it is good to try to put these thoughts and ideas in writing. It is no bad thing to churn one's thoughts around for a time – to transform them into butter, or even cream – but too much churning and they are spoilt, soured or separated, like milk that has been overhandled. I can never make up my mind whether I am latching on to seed-thoughts from the collective unconscious, or whether they are arising from my own unconscious which, we are told, makes up two-thirds of our total consciousness. Both are possible, I suspect. Anyway they both need a good airing.

Thank you for recommending Rupert Sheldrake's book, *A New Science of Life*. Recently I heard a very enlightened Irish priest mention that it was worth reading as it emphasized the fact that the scientific and mystical approaches are blending together, saying the same things but using different terminology. I am interested in Sheldrake's theory of Morphic Resonance and the Morpho Genetic Field which surrounds all forms of life. Experiments have been carried out on monkeys. One was put on an island thousands of miles apart from the rest. All the monkeys were fed sweet potatoes growing on the land. The lone monkey decided to wash the soil off his potato before eating it, and it was recorded that within a certain time the rest of the monkeys were doing the same thing. It is a fascinating hypothesis to think it would only take 1% of the population to effect a change in the world. In lay terms it is the same old adage of religion being caught not taught, a person's presence being the catalyst for this non-verbal process of communication. Plants have been monitored and also been found to react to external stimuli in this way – distance being no barrier; it has been proved that they will respond positively to tender, loving care. Don't we all! Those who have this magic touch with plant life are said to have green fingers, so this invisible interaction with all forms of life has been recognized before the physicists discovered it. It goes to show that there is nothing new under the sun. You and Ralph will remember that Vicky has that 'green' touch with plants. The old walled garden of their new home has not been cultivated for many years, and she is hoping to transform it into a place alive with flowers and vegetables; it will be a splendid home for her bee hives too. How she manages all she does is a wonder to me. Fergus is only two, and Sarah has to be ferried back and forth to school, Brownies, piano lessons etc., and Robert being that much older and away at boarding school has his own ploys in the holidays. In the season she is often busy till early morning bottling, jam-making and freezing fruit and vegetables. More often than not she is also doing some home decorating, even if it is just re-painting an old bookcase for one of the children's rooms. She also manages to read all that I push her way, as well as having time for the many friends who are always dropping in.

Don't you often find words so inadequate, and such a clumsy way of passing on our deeper thoughts and feelings that you desperately try to find words to get beyond the words? The mind boggles and trembles at the misunderstanding that must go on at International Summit meetings, with the language barrier to be reckoned with as well. 'If only – communication could be direct from person to person'; 'If only – thought transference were the norm now', instead of having to wait until we get out of this physical body. But there is no doubt there are signs that this is happening. For example, many people are surprised at receiving a telephone call from the person they were just about to ring. This happened to me last night – Alexander [my son] was dialling me as I dialled his number, and we both thought there was a crossed line and told each other to hang up. Neither of us expected the other to ring, nor did we have a particularly urgent reason to communicate. If we do effect through the media of air waves – the morpho genetic field – perhaps this is our hope for the future, which means that it is our 'beingness' that is important because that is what we are transmitting.

Perhaps we should take more notice of these coincidences – keep a record? It was Dr Winifred Rushforth, the Jungian analyst, who always maintained that 'nothing happens by chance, and that there is no such thing as coincidence'. I am trying to stop myself from saying how EXTRA-ordinary such things are, when in fact they happen all the time. Anyway, it is an insult

15

to my guardian angel when I think how lucky I am when a free parking meter is waiting for my car to slot into on a busy street on Christmas Eve!

So, 'if only pigs had wings' . . . which brings me to a new line of thought. Don't you often feel so limited by the body? Travelling from A to B can be a stupendous effort at times and you get the feeling that so much energy should not have to be expended and that a wish to be at a certain place ought to mean that you are directly there. We are told that there existed (or perhaps still exist) advanced souls in the regions of Tibet who could do just this. Perhaps it is the same power that Padre Pio had? Enough of musing on Lost Wisdom, and let us be thankful that some of the Universal Laws are beginning to be rediscovered.

Janice and I have just heard that our book *Christian Evolution: Moving Toward a Global Spirituality* is to come out in May. Vicky has worked hard correcting and commenting on the proofs.

Looking forward to hearing your thoughts and news, so be in touch soon. May 1984 see us all become more aware and more alive in the real sense. Keep well and keep writing.

With much love to yourself and Ralph,

U.

March 1984

My dear,

Thank you for receiving my garbled thoughts so kindly. Yes, you are right, sometimes we can get closer to someone by writing to them, rather than speaking with them in person. I suppose the personality (that mask we all wear) is less in evidence; it is a more direct in-touchness, from the real me to the real you, as when mind touches mind. Though who the real me is, I don't know. When I look in the mirror and see my outer form I get quite a shock at times, as it doesn't seem to reflect who I feel I am – the image is somehow less. . . does that make sense?

A thought to ponder on – I was reading that we, with our sense of personal identity, our perception of things, and our emotions and thoughts, are the contents of the One Consciousness. So in a sense we are more than what we appear to be; we are a part of the Greater Whole. This seems to touch a bell somewhere deep inside, to do with being a tiny aspect of the God-head . . . ? There is also a theory that only a part of us (our soul) is in this body at this present time, and I must say I so often feel incomplete. The shrinks would say we have to get our male and female principles in balance, our *anima* and *animus* or Yin and Yang, but even after having achieved that, I feel I belong to something greater than the sum of my constituent parts. But back to the clear communication there can be when writing – I suppose the fact that I cannot see your face of surprise, horror or puzzlement as I share my thoughts with you means I am neither inhibited nor encouraged! I just AM; it just IS, so thank you for receiving all this 'stuff'. It is good to know you will discard what is not relevant to you at the moment, so I need not feel I am imposing ideas, and I am grateful for your creative and understanding comments on thoughts that can, as yet, barely be articulated. An understanding friend (one whose empathic scale is high as the therapist would put it) can help to bring to the surface of the mind truths that lie deeply buried and are waiting to be liberated.

A listener can be a very creative sounding board. So thank you for your unconditional acceptance of where I feel I am at the moment. I feel a real inner freedom when you accept these meandering thoughts, which produces a creative effect in helping me to move on. Also you help me to affirm a somewhat shaky identikit of me. If you have heard of the Myers-Briggs personality tests you'll realize that I am what is known as INFP, and they need a good deal of confirming and affirming in order to accept themselves.

It does help to externalize worries, niggles and doubts, and air feelings of anger and resentment. When you give anything a name, identify it, it ceases to have the same power over you – you then have control over it. The ancient Hebrews knew about this, and to let your name be used by another was a sign of great trust; even today you can feel compelled to ask a comparative stranger whether they mind if you call them by their name. By the way, have you noticed that it seems to be the fashion today to change one's name simply because one does not feel like a 'Mary' or a 'Jack'; and you are often asked to do this if you join one of the many present-day cults, but I suspect that it is to make it easier to forget the past and its associations. This could be advantageous if the conditioning imposed had been very destructive and difficult to shed, but I suspect that equally it could be the sign of not facing up to the life one has been given and so become a means of escape into a fantasy world.

I have been giving quite a lot of thought to the structure of my prayer life of late, which no longer means a life apart from everyday life. I no longer want to separate the inner life from the outer life of action, but I wish the two lives would blend together more

18

easily. When that happens I suppose it could be called 'contemplation in action' or the 'sacrament of the present moment'? We were told to be in the world but not of the world, and there lies the subtle difference. When we get lost in our melodramas, sucked into emotional situations where we overreact, we lose our balance and can forget the other world, and the flashes we have been given on the inner-journey. I often know about something, but cannot get it together enough to BE it, actually live it. There is a gap which is often filled with much pain. Perhaps it is similar to the 'dark night of the soul', but I also feel that we must allow ourselves to go right into that void, fear or pain, for it may only appear dark and threatening with our present insight; we cannot yet see what this no-thingness holds for us, for neither the senses nor the brain-bound intellect can penetrate or comprehend this void, as our spiritual perception is still too weak.

Sometimes I long for your less pressured life which would give me more time to meditate. I do admire your discipline – that is where my weakness lies, and I rationalize it by saying to myself that the pressure of living makes it difficult, sometimes almost impossible, to find times of quiet. But, of course, if we really want to do something we can always find the time by spending less time on other things . . . it's just a matter of getting priorities right, I guess.

I also find that the well-known prayer methods and rituals no longer have the meaning they used to have. I want to cry out 'But it is not like that – it is much bigger, deeper, broader . . .' and I find I have nothing to hang on to at times and this can be scary. To find that you cannot see things as you used to leaves you in an uncomfortable state for a while, and I struggle with

19

guilt feelings as well as feelings of aloneness. Nevertheless I have come to the conclusion that it is a healthy
process, as I am driven to acknowledge those hunches
and whispers that hover on the surface of consciousness
and which, in my case, have been trying to gain recognition for years. It all amounts to a fear of letting go
of that which we know and is therefore safe, and letting
oneself be taken into new territories about which we
know very little. But this leap is necessary if we are to
grow. It seems to me that this letting go applies to so
many areas. We all like to be in control of situations,
don't we? I know I have caught myself out by praying
as and when I think I ought to, and having a dry, tiring
time, getting nowhere, all because I am blocking out
the very Energy I am seeking, because I am not allowing
the Spirit to pray through me. And when I cease to try
so hard, and instead spend a few minutes in surrendered
and relaxed readiness, the difference is amazing. Stupid,
isn't it, when all we have to do is respond, be receptive
and allow God to be God in us. One sigh that escapes
from deep within can say it all; it seems to represent a
surrender of our total being and contains all there can
ever be to utter – and more. It is a sigh that feels as if
it contains the yearnings of all humanity. I feel for
mothers with young children who have so little space
to themselves, though I must say Vicky has disciplined
herself to have a 'peaceful' time after lunch which the
children respect, and they are encouraged to be peaceful
too. I admire the way she balances her life with work,
play, fun and a thoughtfulness of things spiritual. It is
all very simple really, yet so difficult to carry out, but
that is partly due to our early training for we were told
to 'try hard', 'nothing comes without effort', etc. Maybe
that's on the material level, but the same does not apply

to the spiritual level. God is bigger than we are, and thank God for that!

At this point I must end – my love as always,

U.

June 1984

My dear,

I apologize for the long silence. The events of life have overwhelmed me for the present. A telephone can be the conveyor of good news, or it can bring news that temporarily shocks one out of one's mind. This happened when my son-in-law rang me to say that Vicky suffered brain damage through lack of oxygen whilst under an anaesthetic for a minor operation, and was on a life-support machine in a critical condition. I now do not believe we can ever anticipate our reaction to any event until we come up against it and know it is for real – the unthinkable has hit us. We may think we have come to terms with death, for we feel sure in our minds that this life is a transitory period, a time of learning, before we are released into a less constricted form of life; and we can understand that it is those left behind who are the ones who suffer, and that our loved ones are alright. We can know all this deeply, but now, after the shock of this tragedy, I am just benumbed. All I can do is ask for courage and patience to ride the storm, so that I can cope with the immediate situation. Death is one thing, but for a young wife and mother to be mentally, physically and irreparably damaged for life is too much to take in – it just cannot be true, or, dreadful thought, could it? So, please, bear with me in my painful numbness; the anguish of the situation is acute and yet we automatically continue to carry out everyday duties – except for the time I went through red traffic lights, which made me realize I am not in control as much as I like to think.

I do not want sympathy; I just want to know how to bear with myself and my feelings. I do not expect anyone to know what a situation such as this is like, unless they have personally experienced it. What I feel at present is that death would have been easier to cope with – more clean cut after the initial shock of bereavement.

To know you are there, a part of this vulnerable, unpredictable existence, when we never know what the next hour will bring, is a help in itself.

Affectionately,

U.

August 1984

My dear,

Vicky's prognosis is not good; another scan showed further deterioration of brain cells. And yet something within me says 'where there is life . . .', but the medical staff just look at me pityingly. Are we really capable of conning ourselves to such a degree, I ask myself? The hardest thing I find at the moment, is the lack of acceptance from the medics that there is a dimension other than the physical. I want to cry out that Vicky is more than just her physical body lying there – much more.

As yet so little is known about the brain, and this is admitted, so this again gives one hope. . . . Experiments have been carried out on rats and mice which show that healthy cells do compensate for damaged ones, so why not in this case . . . ? Hopes are continually raised, only to be dashed by the next negative report. Surely it cannot be wrong to have hope? Anyway it comes in spite of me and of adverse reports. But this continual shifting from hope to despair and back again to hope, is taking its toll on everyone. There is no certainty to hold onto, to keep us anchored, to do anything positive about – there is just the feeling of being totally helpless, and how difficult that is to live with when one longs with all one's being to do something. . . . Life in the world flows on remorselessly, and I feel as if I am being dragged helplessly along within its stream.

Sorry I cannot end more cheerfully but that is how life is.

My love,

U.

November 1984

My dear,

I have returned to the Jesuit College in North Wales, to continue the work of retreat-giving, and I shall make flying visits to Edinburgh on the break days. Although I hated leaving Vicky lying in hospital I know she has Angus, who travels up and down most days when work permits, and the girls and other members of the family are always around, and the many kind friends are frequently popping in, filling her room with an abundance of flowers. We do feel that at the times when she seems to be present, she gives and receives, but it is a new and unusual level of communication. There are too many people picking up this non-verbal communication for it to be a figment of the imagination. One day she will have so much to tell us.

The work I am involved in here during the three-month course on Apostolic Spirituality is based on individually guided thirty-day retreats founded on the *Spiritual Exercises* of St Ignatius Loyola. It is amazing to think that a sixteenth-century man should have had such insight into the human psyche. There can be no doubt that the wisdom came from the centre of his being, from the deep interior life he lived in the spirit; maybe we have to relearn that intuitions can be wiser than our brain-bound intellect.

I also believe in the importance of the person-centred approach – the one-to-one encounter – especially today when the person is in danger of becoming a number bereft of individuality with its own particular needs. The psychotherapist with a spiritual dimension to his or her life often has more to give to those searching for a broader meaning to life than the clergy can offer. I wish those who work in the religious field would acknowledge the importance of people discovering who they are, how they tick, why they react in certain ways, what it is that they truly desire in life and what it is that blocks them from it.

Life's important moments are almost always to do with our relationships with each other, so that the sooner we can learn to understand ourselves, the more chance there is of understanding our neighbour. We are told that we cannot know God until we know ourselves. So, it is our own house that has to be put in order before we can look elsewhere, isn't it? When I understand why someone can make me ratty, I find I have that very same irritating fault in my own make-up. My reactiveness is such a giveaway. In the same way, when I respond to goodness and love in a person, or the beauty in creation, the response is coming from the God-part of me. Growth of the God-ness in us is what life is all about surely?

Our work here is certainly not to solve problems; it has been said that when a question is asked, the answer is already known, and all we do is to facilitate the discovery. But in this instant society we all want instant remedies, ready answers, don't we?

I am increasingly finding that too much emphasis on developing skills and techniques does not necessarily lead to one person meeting another at the soul level. The magic of successful therapy seems to take place when one person gets under the skin of the other, without loss of identity. This means totally accepting the person where they are at and not having a judgemental attitude. It seems to be within this interchange of soul energies, or energies from our Higher-selves, that movement can take place within the client, and very often in the therapist.

We can minister to each other in this way, if we are totally open to one another – open to give and to receive. It is a very great privilege to be a part of this exchange, and the reward and joy of witnessing a change, a movement into a new inner-freedom, is beyond describing.

It feels at times as if a process of osmosis is taking place. The result, anyway, is energizing and life-giving, and it is not confined to those two parties locked in this deep interaction, for it flows out and touches others, in the way that the ripples from a pebble dropped into a pond affect the rest of the water. This energy factor is active when two people are communicating at a level beyond the surface level of the personality. It is at this soul level that I feel Vicky communicates. The best way I can describe the interaction is like a giving and receiving of energies from a place that is deep within our psyche, where we are all one, and joined to the Godhead.

Never dare we presume an unconscious person, or one in a coma, is incapable of understanding what is going on around them. And our part is to be as sensitive as we can to any non-verbal communication that might be coming through the person. Both parties are on an equal footing while an exchange of these energies is taking place; no one is greater or lesser in this place where we are one and undivided.

Many have the idea that to work on ourselves is self-indulgent, but when we understand that all we can give to another is our being-ness – nothing more, nothing less – then it is up to us to ensure that what we give is the best we are capable of at that moment. In this sense, work on ourselves is not merely an introspective occupation; we owe it to ourselves, our neighbours and to humanity. People are therapists when they just listen attentively to a friend trying to put into words their innermost thoughts and feelings. This is what I have been doing during the last five months; my good friends here have been the recipients of a flood of grief and anger, yet they have allowed me to feel safe when the dam burst its banks.

You mention your friend, with whom you share your thoughts, is leaving the district to live elsewhere. I feel for you, as it is a lonely journey at the best of times. But it is surprising (or is it?) how the right person appears in one's life, just at the time they are needed – so look out.

With love and thoughts as always,

U.

January 1985

My dear,

Your news of Ralph's death was a sad shock. Although the suddenness of his leaving this life was a tremendous blow to you, you also know it was the manner in which he would have wished to go, but I know that doesn't lessen the sense of loss. My heart goes out to you and I pray you will be given the strength and courage to live through what will be dark and lonely days ahead, and to know – really feel – that Ralph is nearer to you now than he was before. I shall sorely miss the physical presence of a great friend and companion on the Way.

I am glad you touched on the theme of what it is to be truly human. When a person says 'We are *only* human after all', to one who has, let us say, been grieving over a bereavement, that is a most misleading and derogatory remark if you reflect on it. Can't you feel it pulling you down into despair and despondency: to be fully human, surely is to be *more* than human, not *less*? When we allow ourselves to be inordinately sorrowful over a bereavement, and cannot shake off the sadness after the usual time that is rightly given to mourning, it can turn into a selfish sadness, that is directed inwards on ourselves and which in time can lead to pathological depression. It can also show us that, perhaps, we had an inordinate attachment or dependency, bordering on possessiveness, but you, most certainly, never belonged to that category. And yet kind friends will tell us that we would not be human if we did not go on grieving. Albert Nolan in *Jesus Before Christianity* writes: '. . . he [God] has chosen to identify himself with all in a spirit of solidarity and compassion. If this is true of God, then God is more truly human,

27

more thoroughly humane, than any human being.' And: 'In this sense Jesus' divinity is not something totally different from his humanity, something we have to add to his humanity; Jesus' divinity is the transcendent depths of his humanity. Jesus was immeasurably more human than other human beings . . .' And, surely, this is what we are called to be, divinely human? At the time of this family tragedy, I too find that the 'we are only human' attitude is the prevalent one, and it certainly neither strengthens nor comforts me. Those who help to raise me up are the very few who let me see my own selfish sadness, and who help me to remember that we are more than just this physical body, and that our home is not on earth; we are pilgrims, in exile if you like, journeying home. If I could continually recall this to mind it would be of more help to Vicky and her family. Oh, the endless questions that came to mind which no one can answer, although many offer their personal philosophy by way of comfort, and I gratefully take the parts that ring true, which I already know but need to be reminded of again and again, and the rest I leave. Often it is not what is offered that gives the most strength, but the beingness of a person, their quality, that consoles. I touched on that in my last letter, I think, for I am becoming more and more aware of the importance of the quality of being that we transmit.

Don't you find there are times in life when you have to go it alone; alone, because your feelings are unique to your self and your own individual journey, so no one can ever feel exactly what you feel, which is not to say we don't feel one another's pain. I discovered that a good part of suffering lies in having to stay with the mystery, the unknown, although within the suffering I feel, deep down, that 'All is well'.

We have to acknowledge our weak humanity and finite comprehension and hand the situation over to the Great Physician who will show us the perfection in his time. How difficult it is to know that everything is as it should be, perfect for this moment in time, and to affirm 'God in all things', and that we will never be given more than we can bear. What a lesson there is in the helplessness of such a situation. And it is only when we give up that God can take over. There were times when I felt that if I was a more whole person I would naturally be able to heal my daughter; Christ healed the sick and called us to do likewise. I often thought of Mary during those early days of crisis. She is the symbol of humility, which is what is meant by being divinely human, I suspect?

Word cannot convey what it is I want to send you. But may you be given Light, Peace and Courage. For my part, I give thanks that you are 'there'; it helps in my own ongoing time of struggle. You are needed!

With very much love, and so many thoughts

U.

April 1985

My dear,

There is not a great deal to say except that life goes on . . . and on, day follows day and there is no change in Vicky as far as the medical profession is concerned. Those who sit with her regularly detect subtle changes in her inner-being; for example, at times she appears to like you just being beside her, maybe reading to her. I read *The Prophet*, by Kahlil Gibran which was a favourite of hers, and it feels as if she is absorbing what is

29

being read. At other times you can feel she is not with you, although outwardly she may appear to be no different; but you feel you are talking and reading to a blankness.

Her different inner states show through her eyes which are, oh, so expressive. There has been a lot of fear at times – as if she is living through a nightmare, and I find this one of the hardest things to bear. We do feel that the specially prescribed homoeopathic remedies for this state seem to help her ride out her 'purgatorial' experience. The hospital is so good about giving these powders to her, often at times that are out with her more orthodox treatment times, and which mean an extra trip to her bedside. As Vicky cannot consciously swallow or take anything by mouth, they have to be carefully shaken onto her tongue and a watchful eye has to be kept until they have dissolved.

There are also times when she is relaxed and comfortable and seems to be in a place that is far removed from that hospital bed; a place where we, imprisoned in our limited bodies, cannot penetrate – we remain only on the edge of glory, as it were. There was that day I walked into her cubicle and saw, by the rapturous expression in her eyes, that she was far, far away, in a place that was sacred, a place in which none of us have yet been. Her eyes expressed a joy and delight that no words could ever do. And being there, looking at her, seemed to be an invasion of her privacy. It was like a glimpse of reality that didn't yet belong to us.

All we want for her each day is that she remains as peaceful and comfortable as is possible under the circumstances. The two older children, like us all, want to visit her, and why should they be denied their wish, so they are taken in when she is not in a distressed state. Fergus is too young to remember her, so does not go along, because if he does have memories of her they will be happy, normal ones of a child of two years, which it would be a pity to shatter. I must say that to look at the children as they live through this trauma reduces me to pulp. Maybe I am projecting my own feeling onto them too much.

You will, in the past, have heard me talk about two very dear friends, now in their eighties, who helped me through the divorce period. Their greatest contribution was that they allowed me to 'be'; to go through the bereavement of a severed relationship, and the accompanying mess on the material level, without ever ladling out advice on the different problems that would crop up in the course of events. Neither did they sympathize which makes a problem larger by focusing on it, empathize, yes, which made me feel less alone as they walked with me in the tragedy. Don't you find that sympathy only drags you down further into the trauma? It doesn't help you to see life in its true perspective, or discern the wood from the trees. Their enormous support and strength to me was in the fact that they understood what I was going through, on more levels than one, and were truly beside me, indeed with me. It was because of what they were, due to a dedicated life of meditation, that they were able to uphold me in the midst of the fiery furnace I had to walk through – the Fire that purifies – which enabled me to come out the other side a stronger person. Now these two people are once again the greatest support and source of strength to me. When I anguish over Vicky when she has one of her recurrent chest infections, and wonder how long this will go on for, Maisie will say, with such authority, 'You must leave it to Vicky; Vicky knows what she is doing. She will go in her time . . .' And Annie will say: 'There is a purpose in everything. Vicky is doing something that we cannot understand, and for many people.'

It is easy to forget that we are fundamentally spiritual beings, who have to be shaped and moulded as we learn our lessons on the earth plane, and that it is the soul that continues to exist (call it Consciousness, if you wish), and which is strengthened by the tests and trials that are uniquely ours. No one can tread the path for us, but like my friends, Maisie and Annie, they can be beside us, accompanying us on our Journey.

There is a sense in which it doesn't matter what we do, it is the quality of our presence, what we are that matters, and we in the West find that a difficult one, don't we! It is never an either/or situation, for doing comes out of being. Beingness is transmitted into the physical realm and manifests itself in a living situation. The value of the 'doing' will stem from the quality of being, surely?

Meantime, thank you for being who you are, and for sharing my space with me.

All love,

U.

⁓⁓

June 1985

My dear,

I am very sorry to have to write and tell you that I will not be coming to see you as I slipped when taking my dog for a walk, broke my ankle and will be immobilized in plaster for the usual six weeks. It happened so ridiculously easily: my ankle went over on a stone and

I fell heavily, and the damage was done. However some say 'there is no such thing as an accident', or 'nothing happens by chance', so I must take a look and see what this is saying to me – this annoyance with myself, accompanied by a grousy inner frustration. I suspect the message is to be still, both inwardly and outwardly. I know I am not at all good at that. Also I shall have to remember that it is not what happens to you in life that matters, but what is important is what you do with what happens to you, in other words how you react to life. Meantime we will have to continue to be in communication via the postal system.

This may sound odd, but there is not a lot of spare time in the day; it takes time to think out how I am going to move myself from A to B, and that in turn takes a remarkably long time to carry out, and afterwards I have to recover from the exhaustion of the effort. However I have discovered that this way of life is very conducive to living in the now, because all of my attention has to be focused on what I am doing, so there cannot be any dissipated energies as when my mind is on a hundred and one things that have no relevance to the present moment, and from that point of view I feel centred all the time, and that feels good. The Zen Masters have a point here, and certainly put into practice, the 'Sacrament of the present moment'; as Thich Nhat Hanh says in the little meditation book he wrote for Pax Christi, 'When you are washing the dishes, you are not just washing the dishes to get them clean – no, you are washing the dishes!' You are not washing the dishes so that you can have a cup of tea – you are simply washing the dishes, and that is as important as any other act, if you can do it in a state of full consciousness. That is really what I am getting a taste of, and as I said before, that feels good.

How one appreciates the small things that go to make up life; the chance to lie back and look round the room, and appreciate all the nicknacks I have collected over the years: the Iona stones, the shells from some Hebridean shore, the particular postcard I could not throw away, and all the family photographs. That first cup of tea in the morning that can be slowly sipped, gazing out of the window to get the feel of the day. And unhurriedly reading a book – that is a real treat. When you pick up a book you haven't read for several years, don't you often find meanings in it which did not strike you the first time you read it? It makes me realize how we are changing and developing all the time, but like all growth it is hidden and invisible and takes us by surprise. There are so many levels of comprehension – we need to peel away layer upon layer of consciousness; each level is right for the person at that particular moment. The danger is when we stop and rest in our present layer and declare we have found the Truth: We now have it all wrapped up and are nice and secure again, thank you. It is then that we crystallize and freeze our concepts and are unable to make further forward movement. Anyway, right now I am so fascinated by this enlarged perception which creeps into us imperceptibly that I desperately want to reread all my old favourites, and I don't think there is going to be time in this life! That is really a form of lust, I tell myself, or to put it less dramatically, greed, but, it's the same. I think St Ignatius might call it an 'inordinate attachment' to books, and the Buddhists would say it is a desire that has to be purified so that in the end we become desireless. Both are right, because we have all knowledge within us and must learn to look within, and listen to hear how it all is, and if we continually rely upon external teachings we shall never discover this, and it will prevent a natural unfolding of wisdom. I am very good at preaching to myself you will have noticed.

Why do we allow ourselves to be ruled and pressurized by the clock? How many times in the day do I say 'I must get on', whatever that may mean. Where do I think I am going? There is never time to do what I want to do. I am constantly tearing through all the things I don't like doing, and if there is time at the end of the day, I'm too tired to do the things I like to do. So knowing I can't do any of the 'oughts' for a time gives me a great sense of liberation within my physical confinement. The release of tension is amazing when there is no time-pressure, when I let my meditations simply happen, rise out of some place deep within, then it is not I, but it feels as if another has taken over and is praying through this 'I'. I daresay I would jib at my immobility if I knew it would never end, so I can appreciate the frustration you sometimes experience when your hip is playing up, and the wheelchair is not as mobile as you would wish. Although you so rarely mention your own incapacity, I shall certainly be more aware of your day to day circumstances, and what it is like to have one's independence taken away.

I have discovered I am not a good receiver; I suppose being in the role of a mother with all that this entails, has meant that there have not been many opportunities to be at the receiving end, or maybe at times I have deprived people of the pleasure of giving, which is not such a good thought. I think there probably is a certain pride and lack of humility in all this. I really do want to make the most use of this enforced rest and to take

35

a look at my life, which includes asking myself what is it I want to do in life?

After he was wounded in battle, St Ignatius had time to study his daydreams, which at the beginning were what we would call egocentric, all about performing gallant deeds for his fair lady and gaining much honour. In time these daydreams were transformed until he quite clearly understood that God was asking greater things of him, for the good of many as opposed to the few, but ultimately for the good of the Whole, which as you know was embracing a Religious life and eventually forming the Society of Jesus; and today it seems that the Jesuits are among those who are blazing the trail for the future growth of man in God.

It all goes to show that we dare not dismiss our daydreams lightly, especially if they have been with us over the years, so do encourage those you meet to take a look at what it is they secretly have always had an urge to do or be, and to ask for enlightenment on the matter. As the old Irish saying goes, 'Take time to dream – it is hitching your wagon to a star'. Meanwhile wish me God-speed as I try to read the map of my life.

The news of Vicky remains unchanged. I am in daily touch with the hospital or with Angus and the family who visit her, and the news is always that her condition remains the same. That phrase 'there is no change', however kindly and gently it is said, is like a punch in the solar plexus and the stone that has lain in one's heart for a year gets larger and heavier each time those words are spoken.

Our 'summer' was last Friday, a glorious day, and one to be remembered. I'll be in touch soon.

With much love,

U.

September 1985

My dear,

Thank you for being so totally with me in this travail. Yes, it is a vigil, and although we cannot fully comprehend it, ultimately, I am sure it will be seen to be a blessed one. As you so rightly say, the hardest part is in the loss being so long drawn out, for it is something one never gets resigned to, and hope is never entirely absent, no matter what the medical authorities might say about the condition of the brain. So little is known about the function of the brain cells and of different states of consciousness; for instance it is well known that unconscious patients may hear and understand what is being said around them, and the nurses are told to assume the patient hears everything and to talk to them normally, always telling them what they are about to do.

There is so much one wonders about; we know Vicky's soul or spirit is still here on earth, but is her consciousness the same as yours and mine? Our consciousness is limited and constricted by so many variables – chiefly by our conditioning of who we think we are and what we look upon as the important issues in life. The scientists tell us we normally walk around in a Beta state of consciousness, whereas when we meditate or pray we go into an Alpha state, or a Delta state when we go very deeply into sleep and meditation, so it seems as if it is anyone's guess in which of these states an unconscious person would be in. Sometimes I think there is a form of communication going on when just sitting silently beside her bed. It is a felt awareness, too intangible to put into words, but I am left with a sense of peace after a visit, and as a friend said, 'I often wonder who is visiting whom?' There is no doubt that

37

Vicky draws people to her, and they find it hard to leave when visiting time comes to an end.

I like your phrase 'taking the vision of a miracle' into prayer – visualizing Vicky well again. I, too, believe in affirming wholeness and harmony; there is a power in positive thinking that can effect change. At the same time the perfection lies in his Will, not our little wills. Our desires are so often about 'this world' things, and have we not been told that the Kingdom is not of this world? When we are still, and enter into that cave within where the Spirit dwells, we are able to resonate with God's desires and thoughts and his Will then becomes our will because we see things more nearly as they are.

One way in which my form of praying has changed is that it no longer feels right to ask for anything specifically, for in a sense it is already there, and we fail to appropriate our inheritance. I am reminded of the father in the parable, saying to the elder son, 'All that I have is yours'. We see such a small part of the whole scenery of life that our judgement of what is needed can never be accurate.

I think you may be right when you say that I may have a touch of the guilt bogey about my praying not being as it should be. Blow these 'shoulds' and 'oughts', they still seem to rear their heads from time to time. Will we ever be clear of the conditioning that has been imposed upon us by our upbringing and society? I guess we have to go on working on ourselves, monitoring our reactions and questioning our motives all through our lives – the traps just get more subtle. Life seems to be a perpetual stripping away of constricting bonds which have been imposed on us. Anyway I shall continue to pray as I can, not as I can't, and enjoy the feeling of liberation it brings. I cannot help feeling that the

Institutional Church has a lot to answer for in the way it has allowed its members to have feelings of guilt; by encouraging this it enabled the Church to wield power over the people. We need to be taught how to listen to our conscience, or still small voice within; this would help people to tune in more sensitively and become more aware of what is right or wrong, and to take responsibility for their actions. Living with a guilt state is not healthy for anyone, and infects the spiritual, mental and physical parts of a person. It stunts spiritual growth, keeps the mind going round and round in uncreative circles which may lead to depression, and attacks any weak spot in the physical body. I think of my migraines when the inside of my head feels like a boiling kettle with the lid tied down!

I know I sat on my own beliefs for too long. I was afraid to be true to what was surfacing from deep within for fear of being called a heretic. The result was I got stuck in my cancerian shell and my game of pretence. When I discovered that there were many others with similar beliefs, the feeling of liberation and inner-freedom knew no bounds and I took off, came alive. This says more about me than I like to admit. Being true to myself is something I have always had to struggle with. We do not need to be told what is good or bad for us, as we all have an in-built voice that can tell us what is right or wrong in each particular situation, whether it be that we cannot stomach egg yolks as they make us sick, or whether a special relationship is right or wrong, for although it may appear to be wrong in the eyes of the world, we can know, from that deep centre within, that it is good – that God is in it, and that to deny it would be going against 'Good'.

It is the knowingness that comes from this inner place

that we have to learn to trust; I can so easily get thrown back into, and immersed in, this world's thinking and opinions. Surely, our criteria for right or wrong is always to make sure that whatever we do or say will harm no one? What we have to learn is how to be still and get in touch with, and listen to, that inner voice. When we practise that inner-stillness, we contact the life of the Spirit which frees us from needless and harmful conflicts and tensions in life, the presence of which can block our way to God. I am learning that we also have first and foremost to give ourselves absolution, forgive ourselves, rather than receive absolution via an external channel.

Let us pray for each other,

Love, U.

December 1985

My dear,

Just to let you know that there is still no radical change in Vicky; she has her good days and her bad days, and neither we nor the hospital staff know what is going on at these times. The nursing staff are truly dedicated and give her so much care and kindness, and I am always very touched by the way they treat her as a person who is loved and valued. Yesterday I overheard the cleaning lady tell a nurse, who had newly arrived on the ward, that when the children came in to see their mother to be sure to put 'the hyacinth blue nightie on Vicky as it is the one that she always looks so nice in'. It is this lady who always sees that the best nighties are washed and ready for special visits like this. The same attention is paid to the tapes that are put on for her.

They are so carefully chosen for her ears. Though, I must admit that I once went in to find the radio blaring away and I vowed I'd write a codicil to my will that if I ever became unconscious I would never wish to be subjected to such a racket. It is these small details that give away the genuine care that the ward staff feel towards Vicky and which means so much to us. Twice I went to see the moving film 'ET', which showed so poignantly that nothing can replace love when healing is needed, and now I am having a glimpse of it in action.

As the months go by (it is eighteen months now since the accident) I am more and more aware of a form of communication taking place at a level other than the spoken. The proof for me that it is not imaginary is that there are times when Vicky is simply not there, not with us, in the same way that she does not respond when asleep.

There is a student nurse who is assigned to bathing Vicky daily and while she goes about her nursing duties she chatters to her as she might to her best friend, for she tells me she feels a response which is warm and affirming. Kathleen assures me that when she tells Vicky her problems or shares her joys, Vicky understands – is with her in a way that feels real. When Kathleen was on holiday she went back to her home in Ireland to try and make peace in a painful family rift. She knew it would take more courage than she felt she had in order to face the storm. When the confrontation with her family actually took place, she said she felt the presence of Vicky so strongly, helping her, and indeed the results of her attempts at reconciliation worked in a wonderful and surprising way. All of this may sound trivial but I can assure you that it was a complex situation that had been affecting the family for some time.

41

It is hard to write what I want to convey to you about this other level of communication which is going on between Vicky and people who are close to her (not necessarily the family). Normally when I write to you I can say what is in my heart and mind; no editing goes on, no inhibitions are present. I am reminded of words on a card sent to me:

> Oh the comfort the inexpressible comfort of being safe with a person, having neither to weigh thoughts nor measure words, but pour them all right out just as they are, chaff and grain together, knowing that a faithful hand will take and sift them, keep what is worth keeping and then with the breath of kindness blow the rest away.

All the same, for the first time, a part of me wonders if I should hold back. Partly because it will be difficult to find words, and partly because what I want to share with you is not my own personal experience. However, I will try as it would be unnatural for me to keep anything from you.

To give an example of what is happening with people who are not physically at her bedside, I will tell you about a letter from a friend of both Vicky and myself. Alma has been travelling up to Edinburgh from the Borders to massage Vicky's feet. She is trained in what is known as 'Metamorphic Technique', which is a gentle massage on the spinal reflex of the feet, the spine being the main connection to the organs of the body. The gentle pressure gets rid of blockages while the person relaxes, and this enables the life force to flow unhindered and healing can take place where it is needed. Practitioners do not 'impress' themselves upon the person, they don't get involved, but remain detached because the vital force of each person is far wiser than that of the practitioner. It allows people to move to whatever space they really need to be in. The following is an extract from a letter Alma wrote to me:

> The other day I was talking to Vicky while I was doing her feet and I became aware of how bright and wise her eyes were and how tightly locked she was in her body. It was quite a shock when she jumped several times during the massage and tried to make sounds. [Vicky cannot move or use her vocal chords.] It is always a great privilege to be with her at these times. At home, when meditating, I hold her in the Light and yesterday I was sitting by the fire when I heard her voice – so distinctively Vicky's voice – clearly speaking to me. She said, 'Thank you very much for all you are doing for me.' I got quite a surprise as this hadn't happened before and then I thought it would be nice to have a conversation with her and I asked her why she remained in a coma. Vicky replied that it was because she couldn't make up her mind whether or not to stay on earth or move on. I suggested that it would be a good idea to come to some decision for the sake of the family; and that a friend had told me that people in a coma are in a sort of tunnel and can see the possibilities at both ends, and can hear the doctors and nurses and friends talking but cannot reply. It must be very frustrating for them. Vicky gave a sigh which seemed to say yes, I know, but I'm still very unsure. Then she moved away. . . .

Another friend, Janice, has had similar experiences, of which I'll tell you later. These genuine incidents are

43

suggesting to me that our true self is pure consciousness, which includes our uniqueness and personality traits; this consciousness can be anywhere, at any time, and is certainly not limited to the physical body. It also suggests that we continue to have life, and are still inhabiting the same space, no matter what frequency we are operating on. Sometimes it is as if I cannot get properly tuned into the appropriate channel. It feels as if only a small adjustment would do the trick, but I am unable to make that adjustment. There is certainly more going on than I can grasp at the moment, and I think I have to try and be more aware and sensitive to these areas.

Will write again, e'er long.

All love,

U.

≈≈≈

February 1986

My dear

Last week, for me, was an eventful one. I feel it was also significant for Vicky but in ways we cannot comprehend at present. An Indian Sister (Jayanti) and her Superior, Dadi Janki, made a special visit to the hospital to see Vicky. I first met them in London at the congress of 'A Global Co-operation For A Better World'.

These Religious sisters belong to a worldwide organization called the Brahma Kumaris, founded in India in 1936. It is now a non-governmental organization attached to the United Nations and works for peace and global co-operation, as well as offering spiritual education. I was at once struck by the sisters' spiritual insight and wisdom, along with their depth of vision.

They spoke with an authority that felt to me as if they had their roots in eternity. They had a healing presence and it was because I was so aware of this quality that I asked if they would come and visit my daughter in hospital. Their visit brought healing and comfort to me and also confirmed thoughts I had about the possibility of another form of communication that I was sure was taking place between Vicky and those who visited her.

Let me try and tell you, as briefly as possible, what their philosophy is about. They believe the soul works through the human body, even if the physical functions are impaired; that the soul is still very much alive and fully conscious, even though the brain may be damaged. This, to me, is an indication of the continuity of the soul and the eternal nature of the spirit. When I am sharing at a deep level with a friend I call that a soul-level meeting, but Sister Jayanti is saying it doesn't have to be verbal communication. There are other frequencies, like radio wave lengths, that we can pick up when we are silent and less identified, or caught up, with the physical and material aspects of the world. Lately there have been some good documentaries on television, dealing with near-death experiences and giving evidence that the soul, our consciousness, has an existence or life of its own and can be fully itself outside and apart from the body. So there is more to us than just this physical body which we wear like a garment until it becomes worn out and is no longer needed.

Now let me give you some extracts from a letter Sister Jayanti wrote after their visit:

> We find that many more people today are realizing that when there is a closeness of relationship because of love or maybe because of a deep

45

connection there is in working out a task together, these things bind us together and we can communicate soul to soul through our thoughts and vibrations as much as through physical means. I do believe that the individual soul can communicate directly and silently with God without needing to go to a church or a temple. In my language we describe this as *yoga*, which means union or communion with God. When the soul explores this union with God then the communication they have with other souls is also a very deep and meaningful one. One of the reasons for the superficiality of the West is that generally speaking people don't commune with God and so our exchange with each other as human beings also lacks depth. In one sense it is purposely kept to a superficial exchange because we are scared of being too close to each other, as this will entail our being vulnerable and open.

Dadi Janki felt that Vicky was in a state of closeness to God; there were no barriers around and as the two of them came close on a physical level so they were also able to come closer on a higher level. For me it was not just a meeting between these two souls, it was also a meeting of two souls in the presence of God. I was aware of light at the time – it was as though the whole room was ablaze.

The whole area of how souls communicate and relate to each other and to God is, in a sense, an 'other worldly' dimension which is absolutely real. Very many people either ignore it, or dismiss it, but when something unforeseen like this happens they are touched by it and made aware of the existence of this other dimension.

Today, especially in the fields of science, medicine and technology, we are overwhelmed by the physical aspect of existence. But we do seem to be at a turning-point. There's a real change happening, particularly in medicine, and many more people are beginning to acknowledge the reality of other dimensions. For instance in *Newsweek*, which is very much part of the Establishment, there was an article which dealt with the whole concept of mind/body, body/mind interaction. 'As you think so you are', so if you think in a positive way then this influences your body and makes it strong and healthy. Medical science is now confirming this – and the amazing power of thought is being acknowledged and recognized.

It must have been particularly hard for everyone in Vicky's family to comprehend why she had to leave them as she did but perhaps it helps to see life as a drama that unfolds. One scene finishes and another begins. In this analogy the soul is actor, the physical body is the costume and the world is the stage. So, here we have an actor playing a role, very very beautifully, with a lot of love, talent and creativity, as Vicky did – playing that role, in connection with these other souls who were the immediate family, but the scene finished earlier than anticipated. If we can look at life with a sense of detachment, we can begin to understand our life-stories. However, the concept of detachment is not well appreciated, because it is interpreted as being cold and clinical. In fact it is not, as there is a lot of wisdom in it. If I'm emotionally involved in something, I am too entangled to be able to see anything clearly. I am the actor and I play my role, but I also have to be able to step back from the stage and become the detached observer, watching the whole scene. In that state my vision isn't narrow and I can see things in a much broader perspective.

Everyone finds it immensely difficult to let go, to rise above emotions rather than merely mastering them, so that they are transformed. We find constantly that when things are changing we don't want them to change, we hold onto them and want them to remain exactly as they are. We find this in nature; for instance, flowers are beautiful, but they have a certain lifespan and when the beauty of the flower fades and wilts there's another stage. There are also the seasons, everything moves in cycles and seasons and it's very difficult for us to flow along with them. It requires a great depth of maturity to be able to acknowledge and accept this. Life is constantly on the move, it's a constant process of change. My body isn't still; every moment its cells are going through a dynamic process, every part of me is changing. My own personality is being influenced by the ebb and flow of all the things around me, and yet we find change so difficult to accept.

I know you have heard all this from me in the past but I find it exciting and affirming when it is spelt out by others!

There are three reactions to change. The first is that we don't want any change to take place; we want to hold onto the things of the past and so we fight to stop the change happening. The second is that we don't know what to do when change occurs and so we are saddened by a sense of loss because there's something within us that is dying. The third is to embrace change, and this is the only way to be able to move along with life. It's like the water that flows. If it doesn't flow, if it stands still, it will stagnate. So life, like the water, has to keep flowing and I have to find my point of stillness within me. This point of stillness is my own state of stability even as everything around me changes. This is particularly true of relationships. It's like a mother and her son; the mother will want the son to be the same as he was 20 years ago and she will want to continue to have the same relationship. But of course it is impossible. The wise mother is the one who lets go and accepts that her son has moved, and finds love in a changing relationship.

Generally we forget the consciousness of the soul and what we have to do is to come back to that awareness. When there is a feeling of soul-consciousness, there is an awareness of the eternal self. We should be able to see the eternal realm and relate to each other as if we were in an eternal relationship.

One of the things about the communication between Dadi and Vicky is that on an external level here were two people who were literally continents apart in terms of language, culture and age. Dadi is an Indian woman who has no relationship on any physical level with this other individual and yet what was enabling that communication to happen when they were together was a relationship that was eternal, a connection that was beyond this body – a communication which is based totally on soul-consciousness. And the lesson that I would learn from this experience is that even now as we engage in our activity in this life, it is possible for us to

49

have this eternal relationship. We can discern a light and peace which can be shared, and if we can forget about the material things, we can avoid the blocks that occur on the material plane. With Vicky there were no blocks because her consciousness was able to go beyond our present level of understanding to a place where communication happens instantly.

If you look at all the different advances that have been developed in the world, one of the only areas that we haven't delved into deeply and which we have yet to explore and understand is that of the mind – the last frontier. I see that this is now happening. For me, the mind is part of the soul because it's the most active and instantly discernible manifestation of the soul. It is distinct from the brain and is perhaps like a bridge between the soul and the brain. The brain is part of the body. It is like a computer system and the thoughts of the mind manifest through the rhythms of the brain. What happens in meditation is that you are able to come to a state in which the mind is very alert and yet the brain rhythms are equally in a state of rest. On an ordinary physiological level this is something that is very strange. As a meditator, Dadi Janki was involved in a laboratory experiment in San Francisco, where they were testing biofeedback; she was given some calculations to do and it was discovered that her mind was totally alert although her brain was registering Delta, which is the rhythm of deep sleep. This detachment of mind from body was due to her training in meditation. In a situation such as Vicky's the mind can be perfectly alert although it can not register through the vehicle of the brain.

I see that many things are happening in the world today which are making us aware that there's a lot more depth to the human experience than we could have imagined some years ago. For instance, we are coming to the point when we are realizing the oneness of the planet and our responsibility as a whole global family towards it. It has taken disasters like Chernobyl and the potentially life threatening gaps in the ozone layer to make us realize that we have to work together. Again, things like the discovery of the connection between the immune system and our emotions, feelings and health, opens up a whole new perspective. If we keep our mind in a healthy state then there's going to be a better physical health because the immune system depends upon the quality of our emotions and thoughts. Statements like these would have been laughed at even five years ago, but today ideas related to ecology and health are part of the growing total awareness which includes a recognition of the spiritual qualities of life. People are no longer satisfied with just physical achievements, they are also concerned with quality, with feelings. There does seem to be a shift in consciousness, indicating that we are now ready to emphasize the non-physical aspect of life as contrasted to the material/physical aspects. This is happening more and more, and the story of Vicky and how communication can move beyond the limitations of the physical level, will help that growing awareness.

I do apologize for bombarding you with so many thoughts and theories, but for me they have a profound ring of truth. So much of it makes 'soul-sense' to me

51

and that in itself is a comfort. I have not found much solace within the teachings of the Institutional Church; indeed we are not encouraged to look beyond this life, although we know it is transitory and that we are made in the image of God who is spirit. We profess to belong to one Body, that we are all one, yet find it hard to incorporate all of humanity, whatever the race, creed or culture. That Body must surely include all of humanity as well as those who have 'gone home'?

There can be no separation within the oneness of creation, so let us rejoice and believe.

With love from one to one,

U.

June 1986

My dear,

Vicky passed on to the Greater Life, very peacefully on 24th May. Philippa, Georgina and I were on the Island of Iona when a call came from Angus to say she had taken a sudden nose-dive and that this was not of the same pattern as her recurring chest infections. This came as a shock, as when I left her three days earlier she had been as physically well as she had ever been. We had been reading *Mr God, This is Anna* – a book she particularly liked and we felt she was enjoying it. I told her where we were all going, and that Father Gerry Hughes and I were taking a retreat and I got a faint impression that she was pleased about this. She had met Gerry when he came North to give a series of talks to local friends, but she had to leave before the end in order to go into hospital. I knew she loved Iona and I said we would take her with us in our hearts and that she would be with us in spirit.

It was a sad and strange experience to help someone out of this world whom you had brought in and nurtured, but it was also a great privilege to be part of the new birthing. The morning before she died I was very aware of a host of Beings of Light in a semicircle above her bed. During the day they came closer, until at the end they seemed to be almost within reach of her, waiting to embrace and enfold her in love and care, as with a smile on her lips, her soul took the final step. Her room was ablaze with light and alive with love and I, myself, felt held in a strong peace – even joy.

I knew Vicky was alright for she radiated a peace that is not of this world. I felt the peace I experienced was but a pale reflection of hers. It is those left behind who have to live with the loss, and who need care, isn't it? I do not doubt that she and Ralph will get together and continue to share their love of plants. The thought of his presence with her gives me a deeply happy feeling. Let's pray for them both.

I was very aware of Vicky around me for a few days after she left us. Sometimes it was in the form of a fresh, flowery perfume. At other times I felt a nudging, as if she was wanting to attract my attention. At first I was far too preoccupied to stop and pay attention, but one day it was so strong that I was stopped in my tracks and made to go to the telephone to ring Angus. As I dialled the number I really was not sure why I was ringing, except I vaguely thought it was to do with funeral arrangements. Then with a suddenness that was like a jolt it came to me that Vicky would like donations sent rather than flowers. But donations to which organization? Then 'my' thinking took over and I wondered if it was to do with brain-research, and at that point I received a definite 'No' – a shut-off feeling. At this point the telephone was answered by Angus' brother, who said Angus had left the house two minutes earlier to catch the post so as to get the notice of the funeral arrangements into the paper. My heart sank. I felt I had failed Vicky; I had been too slow in recognizing her nudge; it was too late now. Then David said, 'Oh, hold on a second, I think this is Angus back', as indeed it was – he had forgotten something. As I talked with Angus about the idea of donations, the words 'for the Homoeopathic Research Trust' came into my mind. He replied that it was a good idea as she was a life member of that Trust – and I had not known this. I was left with a feeling of having done what had been asked of me. Maybe I'll share the other incidents at a later date when I'm feeling less fragile.

My love as always,

U.

* * *

July 1986

My dear,

The day I dreaded is over. Vicky's funeral took place in a tiny pre-Reformation kirk standing amongst trees. Only the immediate family were there; not the children as they are coming to the memorial service. To begin with the unreality of it all kept me at a distance – I felt far removed from what was about to take place.

It was at the sight of the coffin that I crumbled and was drawn into the depth of our 'this world' thinking, and I mentally blanked out. Later, when I came to, I heard the minister saying, 'and all things shall be made new . . . the world of the past has gone'. At that moment I felt a peace and lightness that was totally contrary to the depth of grief I had experienced a few minutes earlier. The switch of mood did not come from within myself. At the same time as these words were read out by the minister, the birds began to sing as if their throats would burst. Minutes before they had been chirping in the way they usually do on a warm, sunny May afternoon. My eyes were drawn to a window pane high up to the right, where I could see the bright green of newly opened leaves of a beech tree, which was where the birds seemed to have gathered. There, silhouetted against the green tapestry of leaves I 'saw' the translucent but totally whole figure of Vicky. She was so happy, and seemed to be pointing me to the words 'the old order has passed away'. Then followed silent communication when she 'told' me that her work now was to help people through the transitional stage, from the old order to the new. I got the impression she was telling me to 'come on', respond, that we here have to do our part in bridging the old and the new, and she was joyfully, oh so joyfully, about to do her part from her newly-found sphere. Implicit in her message was the truth that the work is the same wherever we are. We are called to be co-creators in building the Kingdom, all are involved in participating in bringing in the New Creation – the New Age. The veil is getting thinner. There will be a new heaven and a new earth: the world of the past has gone; now the whole of creation is being made new. The impact of the sense and truth of all this was so great on me that I walked out of that little kirk, filled with a peace and joy that bore no relation whatsoever to my feeling of utter desolation of twenty minutes earlier. And I still live with the sense of urgency, along

55

with an increased sense of responsibility to respond to Life – to God – to say 'YES' – go *with* the evolving of creation.

God's presence has always been with us; it is we who have been blind and deaf and unable to get in touch with it. Now it is begging to be allowed to be recognized, and Vicky is one of the many messengers from the other side who reiterate the Good News.

Please pray that I have the courage to respond – to be more aware and to pay attention to the little things in life which are as much signposts as the seemingly bigger events.

With my love,

U.

August 1986

My dear,

How I wish you had been with us on the 1st of July. You would have approved, I am sure. Vicky's Memorial Service was all we intended it to be; a time when everyone who had known her could participate in an act of thanksgiving for her life and her friendship. It was such a real time; everyone dropped masks and roles and you could feel the spectrum of emotions which were as varied and colourful as the masses of flowers with which they mingled. At the same time there was a togetherness, a one-pointedness that was reflected in the reading Angus gave from *The Prophet*, on 'Speak to us of Joy and Sorrow'.

Then a woman said, Speak to us of Joy and Sorrow
And he answered:

Your joy is your sorrow unmasked.

And the selfsame well from which your laughter rises was oftentimes filled with your tears.

And how else can it be?

The deeper that sorrow carves into your being, the more joy you can contain.

Is not the cup that holds your wine the very cup that was burned in the potter's oven?

And is not the lute that soothes your spirit the very wood that was hollowed with knives?

When you are joyous, look deep into your heart and you shall find it is only that which has given you sorrow that is giving you joy.

When you are sorrowful, look again in your heart, and you shall see that in truth you are weeping for that which has been your delight.

Some of you say, 'Joy is greater than sorrow', and others say, 'Nay, sorrow is the greater'.

But I say unto you, they are inseparable.

Together they come, and when one sits alone with you at your board, remember that the other is asleep upon your bed.

Verily you are suspended like scales between your sorrow and your joy.

Only when you are empty are you at standstill and balanced.

When the treasure-keeper lifts you to weigh his gold and his silver, needs must your joy or your sorrow rise or fall.

It was impossible to separate the sadness and the gladness. The line between the two was as thin as a cobweb. I read an extract from *Letters written by the Abbé de Tourville:*

We must think of those who have died as alive and joyful and we must rejoice in their happiness, remembering that we are in close and constant communion with them – our life only separated from theirs by the thinnest of veils. We must remember, too, that this does not separate us from either God – our eternal joy, who more than makes up all that we lack – or from the companionship of those who are with God in infinite time and space. Let us be brave and keep the eyes of our Souls wide open to all these realities: let us see clearly around us those things which others only care to see dimly. The life of man is by no means limited to its short passage through this world. Death is only an illusion which hides from us the continuing development of life. Interior changes gradually make us realize that, in spite of all our alterations, we are indeed immortal, with a life, an endless activity, which death does not cut short: far from it.

Whatever time therefore, we may have lost in this world through circumstances which have checked our activity, is a small matter compared to the life without end which dwells in us and which will easily catch us up later on.

Life limited by death? Nonsense. That is a great mistake. Death hardly counts; it is a mere appearance; we already have eternal life and that reflection should give us great tranquillity, as those who feel themselves to be eternal.

Do not therefore be afraid of death. It is the flowering of life, the consummation of union with God.

I chose to read this because it is what I deeply believe and I hoped other people would be able to share those thoughts, not so much for consolation as for the fact of their reality.

Phillipa read from St John's Gospel, chapter 14, verses 1–6, and gave her own personal prayer which was one of the most moving parts of the service and touched everyone.

The Bishop of Lewes gave the address; you will remember Father Peter who married them. This is some of it.

> We have all seen it – a shaft of sunlight streaming out of a clouded sky, gliding across a mountainside, lighting up the rocks and shrubs as it races over them. It is soon gone, but it is a brilliant moment in its effect and in its hope.
>
> That is a picture for today and as I recite a poem by the Welsh poet and Anglican priest, R. S. Thomas, I want you to think of Vicky.

THE BRIGHT FIELD

> I have seen the sun break through
> to illuminate a small field
> for a while, and gone my way
> and forgotten it. But that was the pearl
> of great price, the one field that had
> the treasure in it. I realize now
> that I must give all that I have to possess it.
> Life is not hurrying
> on to a receding future, nor hankering after
> an imagined past. It is the turning
> aside like Moses to the miracle
> of the lit bush, to a brightness

that seemed transitory as your youth
once, but is the eternity that awaits you.

Vicky is the illuminating sunlight and she knew how to
live fully in its light in whatever she did whether it
be fishing with the children, bee-keeping or home-
making . . . it is this ability to *live* that cleanses the
darkness.

Life is the secret heart of the Gospel. What stands
out about Jesus is that he is fully alive, not a gliding
pious figure, but someone who has time to gaze on
a lily. Everything around him came to life.

Vicky sensed that this real life is the great gift of
the Holy Spirit, the *living* Spirit of life. Sophisti-
cated Christians talk much of the Spirit – but the
childlike who truly see and breathe in the Spirit
quite simply love God and live abundantly.

The clue to that awful accident which crippled
her movement in and response to life, but not to
her true life, is the great Christian mystery in which
Christ transferred his teeming life to us – by his
death. The way of death preserves our freedom
and humanness. In remembering Vicky, our human
seeing alone cannot dictate what is true because it
is finite, but the work of dying is both finite and
infinite; it is boundary work and Victoria was
always pushing back the boundaries of seeing and
responding. Perhaps those who search in untra-
ditional ways have no boundaries, only horizons
to strive freely towards; and with Vicky this was
reflected in her homoeopathic interest, the Wrekin
Trust, editing her mother's book, and even in child-
hood when she bet a friend that she could ride from

the east to the west door of Harrods on her bicycle
– inside – and she did!

We rejoice that in her accident she drew the
flashing sunlight over the rocks and roughness of
the mountain of darkness and brought in the won-
drous Light of Christ.

Let me finish with a verse about such a person:

> She did not let the world go by
> But drew the rainbow from the sky
> And with her craft of palette knife
> She stroked rich colours onto life:
> Strong reds where flames of hearts had cooled;
> And tender blues where passions ruled;
> Yellows where springs of love had dried;
> God's green on wounded countryside.
> She did not let the world go by,
> But drew the rainbow from the sky.
> Hers were the colours of the light –
> That Son which triumphed over night.

The service was full of such beautiful poetry which
spoke volumes but I would like to end by sharing with
you an extract I came across from the writings of
Teilhard de Chardin:

> Illness by its very nature tends to give those who
> suffer from it the impression that they are no use,
> or even that they are a burden. However – the
> world is still building, this idea must be grasped.
> The more we reflect, in the light of lessons to
> be learned from nature, science, philosophy and
> religion, the more we realize that the world is to
> be likened to some organic system, animated by a
> broad movement of growth, special to itself. Over

61

the centuries an all-embracing plan seems in truth to be unfolding around us, something is afoot in the universe, some issue is at stake, some process of gestation and birth, the birth of the spiritual reality formed by the souls of men and by the matter which they bear along with laboriously; the new earth is gathering its forces, emerging and purifying itself.

If the world really represents a conquest still under way, if we are thrown into the thick of the battle, then we can understand that, for the success of the universal effort, pain is inevitable. The sufferers, whatever the nature of their suffering, are the reflection of this austere but noble condition. They are not useless and diminished elements. They are merely those who pay the price of the universal progress and triumph. They are the ones who have fallen in the field of honour.

Thus it is exactly those who bear in their enfeebled bodies the weight of the moving world, who find themselves, by the just dispensation of Providence, the most active factor in that very progress which seems to sacrifice and shatter them.

The sick man, by his apparent inaction, is faced with a most noble human task. No doubt he must never cease seeking cure. No doubt he must employ his remaining strength in what work is still open to him but the sick man should understand that, to the very extent of his sickness, he has a special task to fulfil, in which no one else can take his place – namely to co-operate in the transformation of human suffering. What a vast ocean of suffering is represented by the whole of the suffering at any moment, but what makes up that suffering? Blackness, deficiency, waste? No, we repeat, but rather potential energy. In suffering is concealed, with extreme intensity, the world's power of ascension. In that Day when every man's work shall be made manifest, it may be found perhaps, that none have done Him better service than some of those who all through this life, have been His ambassador in bonds.

I feel very sure that Vicky's suffering, as well as that of the family, can be used to help in the transformation of human suffering, which in turn will help bring to birth the New Man, as the old order becomes the New Creation. I shall not forget those words in the funeral service . . . 'the old order has passed away'. Yes, the world of the past is no longer; we must live in the present, for the present holds the seeds of the future.

Meantime let us continue to pray for Ralph and Vicky.

All love,

U.

September 1986

My dear,

Your last letter said all the things one knows in the head yet finds so difficult to live out. How true it is that although it is a long journey from the head to the heart, it is longer still from the heart to the habits. The more insidious habits are automatic mental reactions; for example we have had it impressed on us that death is the final tragedy, so grief feelings are the instant reaction to death. It does not matter that a part of us knows this is not the whole truth – out of habit we are filled with sorrow. I agree that we should be educated for the transition we call death; to learn that it is actually a passing through a membrane-like substance in order to be freed into a wider, lighter form of life. How restricted we can feel inside this body-form with all its limitations. It was Thomas Arnold, the one time headmaster of Rugby, who replied to a prospective parent's query as to what the school taught, 'We teach that life is a preparation for death, and education is about coming to terms with the greatest moment in our lives'. I believe that today people are asking to have the 'death area' opened up, talked about and accepted as an everyday part of our living. Great interest is being shown in recent television programmes such as 'Near Death Experiences' and 'Is There Something After Death'. I find the topic picked up and spoken about by the people I meet during the course of the day, such as the milkman, postman, shopkeeper or hairdresser – whoever. A friend of mine, a Religious Education teacher of a sixth form, was faced by an alert class who had watched one of these programmes the night before and were eager to talk about this 'death business' rather than stick to their scheduled religious session. They expressed this wish because they knew it was relevant to themselves sooner or later, and most of them had been involved with relatives with cancer; but above all, they sensed a ring of truth running through the television documentary and they wished to be allowed to discuss it further.

A minister of the Church said to me the other day, 'I find I think a good deal about death these days', then hastily added, 'But not in a morbid way'. Those last few words showed the unease he felt in even entertaining such a thought, and he wanted also to assure me that he wasn't a depressive. I found myself replying: 'Morbid? Of course not. It's an exciting transformation, and the only thing we can be certain of in this life.' But I was then left with the feeling that I myself had been labelled as suffering from morbidity, or even of having a death-wish, instead of which I felt I was only accepting the most crucial part of life and saw no need to sweep such an important event under the carpet. Personally, I feel I am still on my Second Journey and haven't yet begun the Third Journey, if there is to be a third. If I live to be eighty, and am still mobile, I shall celebrate the fact that I am on the last lap, on my way home, by dancing an eightsome reel with the help of a wee dram of whisky, maybe!

There are times when I wonder if we are all walking around in a semi-sleep state, and are actually in varying degrees of hell. I feel this especially when I am mixing with frenetic shoppers in our busy towns. Everyone looks so worried, life seems to bear down on them like a heavy crowbar. Plato must have had this idea in mind, over 2,000 years ago, when he wrote about the Cave, where men are imprisoned and believe the shadows they see cast on the walls are the reality. We are still prisoners of our illusions and need to raise our sights and see things as they really are.

I do find the attitude that we don't know and don't need to know about the hereafter is not in keeping with the climate of thinking today. At the time of my own bereavement my help did not necessarily come from those within the Institutional Church (apart from those with whom I was working in Apostolic Spirituality). Help came from those who deeply accepted what had happened – as a tragedy, yes – yet saw within it a purpose, maybe stemming from past lives, but anyway not an accident in the way we would normally think of it. Nothing happens by chance – of that I feel gut-sure. The trouble is, as yet, we see such a very little piece of the great tapestry of Life.

Although a part of me can know, with a deep-felt knowledge, that all I've said to you is true – at the same time it does not prevent me from experiencing the pain and grief of a physical parting, for that is a part of our human condition. Vicky's funeral confirmed that.

Take care. You are still needed,

Love U.

From Janice

November 1986

My dear Mrs Ivens,

Although we have only met a few times I feel I know you through Ursula, who often speaks of you. As you have known her family for so long, I thought I would write to you and tell you The Story from an outsider's angle.

I am sure Ralph would have agreed that the many ~~chanaes affectine~~ ~~Ralph would have said, if we been~~ ~~an~~chors on to externalities, we find that these quickly shift and we are adrift again until we find our anchor-hold within. Such nautical allusions come easily to me as my husband is a part-time sailor and I have known

66

the crucial value of a safe anchor during a storm at sea. When the storm hit Ursula with the news that Vicky had suffered irreversible brain damage, in a secondary way it hit me as well, and I felt a sense of separation from Ursula as we were hundreds of miles apart and it was not possible to hug each other or share a tear. I could only listen and respond as gently as possible, offering the empathy that came from knowing how I would feel if this happened to one of my own daughters. It was hard to believe that just a few weeks previously Vicky had attended the launch of our first book as if she were a breath of fresh country air arrived in London. The anchor inside of me pulled fiercely. How firmly was it set in the quiet confidence that 'All is well, all manner of things will be well'? To know and accept the world as it is without resisting the seemingly negative occurrences and yet, at the same time, to work as hard as we can to put these right, brings a seeming dichotomy that takes the intuition as well as the intellect to resolve. Can events be both right and wrong at the same time?

My first great lesson in this regard and the assurance of the continuity of consciousness from this plane of existence to another, came with the death of my father whom I had always adored. I knew he was ill and being cared for by my sister more than a hundred miles away but I did not realize that his death was so near. My beloved Pop could surely never die? It was during the Confirmation service of my second daughter, while the bishop was confirming her and, in my prayer, I was holding her in the light asking that her life may be blessed, that suddenly my father was 'there'. An incredible awareness of his presence came over me together with an overwhelming sense of peace and joy. I knew he must be dead else how could he be there? But if he was dead then how could I be feeling such joy? Indeed, as I soon discovered, he had just died and in his release must have taken part so joyfully in a family event in which he had wanted to share. His presence stayed close to me for several days as did this amazing awareness of joy. It was almost as if I, too, had been released into a world of radiant light and joy. During these few days my father and I talked together. It was his voice, for sure, but we communed through the mind in a way that can best be described as telepathic.

So, at the time of Vicky's accident, this communing form of communication was not new to me, but it was still with some hesitancy I first encountered her about six weeks after the accident had occurred. I was away from home directing a summer school at Sussex University when I awoke one morning to find her standing beside my bed. I knew it was her. It was her presence, her colour which is a gorgeous mid-blue and her special floral fragrance. 'Please tell Mum that it's alright. It's alright as it is', she urged. How does one convey that over the phone? I mused on it for a couple of weeks, till sitting on a camp bed for a rare rest in our garden I was aware of her again: the message was the same, 'Please tell Mum that it is alright'. The impression I got was that to lie in bed unable to communicate physically, was not the total disaster that it seemed to us from where we are now. Certainly, all along, Ursula had been aware that it would be wrong to hold someone here if it was their time to move on. In fact her equanimity throughout the whole affair was an amazing counterbalance to the natural grief, that, as a mother and grandmother, she was feeling.

My first visit to Vicky in hospital in Edinburgh was both a shock and a pleasure. A shock in seeing just how inert she was compared with the Vicky I had known. A pleasure in seeing how Ursula and all the hospital staff were assuming her consciousness at some level and had filled the room with flowers and taped Scottish music, and also kept her regularly changed into clean pretty nightdresses. Everyone spoke to her just as though she could hear. Could she in fact hear I wondered? Where was her consciousness now – inside her body or outside? How hard to tell. There seemed to be no contact between us at any level.

The following day we drove up to Ursula's cottage in the Black Isle and I was waiting while she shopped in the Post Office at Kessock. Standing overlooking the Firth I became aware of Vicky at my side. It seemed perfectly natural that we should stand and talk together. The impression she imparted to me was that her time in this present state was not wasted; her consciousness was able to travel out of her body to see and understand so much more than she had before. More importantly, it seemed that while she was lying there between this life and the next one, her physical body could act as a bridge between the two worlds. The picture I got was that her spirit was in contact with realms of light and that through the vehicle of her seemingly lifeless body, these other realms could be filtered through into our world. It reminds me rather of osmosis, of a molecular interchange of energy; just as a flame will heat a pan of liquid through an exchange of molecules, so a light of higher frequency can effect and interchange with the earth's vibratory pattern. This seemed to explain so well how some people visiting her came away feeling renewed and uplifted. Her mission, if one can describe it as such, seemed not just to assist the friends who visited her but to be a part in effecting a transition of this world into a new age of consciousness. I realized that she could now begin to perceive how the world might be if we were more closely attuned to spheres of light.

Having conveyed all this to Ursula, my contact with Vicky ceased for a while. Ursula was fully occupied with continuing her work, with her frequent dashes up the M6 to visit Vicky, and with playing her role of comforter to family and friends. When she asked if I would like to join a retreat on Iona that she and Father Gerard Hughes were leading in the spring, I queried whether she would feel up to this. 'Surely', she replied, 'And anyway, it is what Vicky would have wanted. She loved Iona and I'm sure she will be there with us.'

Coincidentally the time of this retreat was to be exactly two years after Vicky's accident. Iona is a special place at any time. A place where the heavens seem to touch the earth more nearly. When one is on Iona it is easy to have a glimpse of Jacob's ladder, up and down which the angels travel bringing a higher consciousness into our world and in return taking our dreams and aspirations to be woven into the gossamer pattern of life. One has, indeed, a glimpse of humanity as being a bridge across which the denser vibrations of physical matter and the higher vibrations of spiritual awareness meet and mingle, each level raising and transmuting the one below. Is this not similar to the idea that Vicky may be acting as a bridge between the two worlds?

At the beginning of the retreat, Vicky was not at the front of my mind as Ursula had assured me that despite many physical ups and downs she was in a stable condition and all was well, in relative terms at least. The retreat started without incident, and the Saturday and Sunday were peaceful and engaging. To have time away to be with oneself and one's Creator, however we may perceive him/her to be, seems a necessity for anyone who is seeking to fix their anchor-hold in the firm grounding of their soul. The week seemed to stretch meaningfully ahead. It was on the Monday that the call came to Ursula that Vicky had taken an unexpected and severe turn for the worse. Ursula was amazingly calm. She felt that Vicky would appreciate our being on Iona and want her to stay, but her other two daughters (who were also on the retreat) decided to leave the next day so that some of the family would be in Edinburgh. That evening we all gathered in the small Oran Chapel near the Abbey to pray. The following day seemed a bit upside down but Ursula was marvellously calm and the retreat continued. She has an amazing way of not burying things but of living through them fully.

By the Tuesday evening it was decided that Ursula would return to Edinburgh next morning and that I would travel with her. At 6.30 a.m. on Wednesday came another call that Vicky was dying and that we must hurry to catch the first ferry of the morning in order to make the steamer connection to Oban.

Once we were on the other side of the water and driving across Mull we began to relax. It was a beautiful morning and we stopped to pick some flowers to take to Vicky. I'll never forget the fragrance of those primroses fresh with early morning dew. They carried the promise of the first morning of a new earth. Somehow these fragrant flowers made a connection. As we got into the car and continued on our way Vicky seemed to be there with us. We were both aware of her at the same time, assuring us that there was no hurry to rush unduly. The conversation continued off and on along the road from Oban to Edinburgh until at one point we burst into laughter. It just seemed so funny that on one level we were rushing to be with a dying daughter while, at another level, she was perfectly well and conversing with us. Which was the true reality we wondered? Driving along the road it seemed we could live in both and learn to be in this world but not of the world. When we arrived at the infirmary it was different. The reality of the hospital scene brought us back to earth.

Recently I saw a video called 'Visions of Hope' which consists of interviews with eight people who have undergone a near death experience. They all speak of how their consciousness was not inside their sick and seemingly dying body, but rather up above watching the efforts of the nursing staff to save them and cope with the grief of their relatives. The message that this excellent video conveys is that if we only knew about the glories of dying we would live more joyfully and without fear. At the time of Vicky's death I had not seen the video, but my own feeling of how it must be encouraged me to communicate with Vicky as being more than a dying physical body. Even so, it was hard to connect the living Vicky who had been conversing with us on the journey, to the Vicky on the bed. Ursula spoke to her so gently, assuring her that it was safe to go on. When she went to speak with the hospital staff, I was left alone and decided that singing might be a good way of connecting. Finding a Scottish hymnal I launched into the few hymns that I knew, 'The Lord is my Shepherd' and 'The King of Love my Shepherd Is'. Their meaning seemed even more profound: 'Though I walk through death's dark vale, I fear no ill, for thou O Lord art with me.' It seems we are accompanied all the way if we are open to it.

We left the hospital quite late and on returning to

Ursula's flat, I went to the bathroom to prepare for bed. I was surprised to hear Vicky saying, 'Thank you for singing to me in the hospital just now'. We then proceeded to have the most amazing conversation. Although chilled and uncomfortable I was apprehensive of losing the connection by moving into my bedroom, but I decided it was worth the risk just to be more settled. There was no need to worry, we continued conversing just as before. We talked about her three children and about my children, just as two mothers might do sitting on a park bench. But this conversation was from a higher perspective for it was as though she could see their life paths clearly and the environments that they needed to fulfil their own purposes on earth.

As I recall our conversation, I find that I am remembering not just the words that she said but also the space behind the words which was conveyed at the same time. It was quite beautiful and confirmed so much that has come to us in recent years through the writings of those in touch with these higher levels of beauty and awareness. She particularly encouraged us to go on with our writing and assured me that she would still be helping us with our next book as she had promised. 'Be surprised at nothing', she said, 'Just do not be surprised'.

I thought you might like to hear all this from a close friend of Ursula's, yet from one who was not emotionally involved. All that I experienced was straightforward and factual and never did I doubt its reality.

I hope Ursula will take me over to see you when next she is south.

Meanwhile with loving memories of both you and Ralph,

Janice

December 1986

My dear,

I've already mentioned my friends, Annie and Maisie, whom I visit regularly in their cottage home, and who have always been a great support in times of trouble. To be with them as they sit either side of the fire in their room overlooking the river Tay, for me is a time of pure contentment and peace; it is a similar experience that I share with you when I come aboard 'Mallard'. We exchange thoughts and feelings about our respective journeys but in the times of silence we seem to share even more deeply and I always come away with joy in my heart and a spring in my step. This is because of who they are – two people living hidden lives of surrender to God, whose work lies in their times of daily meditation. Their lives are a reflection of this dedication which makes them channels of the Christ light. Their gift to the world is themselves.

They told me they prayed for Vicky every day. They said they always had a strong sense that however bad the situation was Vicky knew what she was doing, and was not idle during this time. They used to say to me 'Leave it to Vicky'.

A strange thing happened to Annie on the eve of her 80th birthday, about six months after Vicky's accident. She said she never had a wink of sleep all night. She felt someone wanted to tell her something. She suddenly became aware of Vicky near the window and heard her say, 'Tell Mum that I am working with handicapped children in their sleep state. She'll be quite surprised.'

Annie said that she was certainly surprised by this incident as her thoughts had been on the birthday party that was being given for her the following day. She was quite certain that it was no dream, nor an out of the body experience. She was wide awake when Vicky appeared 'very solidly' in her room. Annie could not contact me as I was working in North Wales at the time. Three days later Vicky was beside her as she washed the dishes. 'You haven't told my mother what I told you. Please do – I want her to know.' Annie then asked her what kind of handicapped children she helped and she replied, 'Both mental and physical, and please tell Mum'. Annie then knew that she had to do all she could to get that message to me.

Now let me tell you my side of the story. As busy and absorbed as I was with my work of retreat giving, one evening I had an urge to ring Annie; maybe she was not too well, or needed something, I thought to myself. Imagine my surprise when I heard what Annie had to say.

After I had been given the message, I must confess, I felt slightly annoyed, or was it hurt? Why had not Vicky come directly to me to tell me that, after all I was her mother? Later I could understand how that would not have been possible as I was so buried in my work and enveloped in all that was going on in the college that I would not have had ears to hear or eyes to see beyond what was in front of my nose. The body metaphors are not inappropriate for I was truly locked into the physical and intellectual realm of 'this world thinking', and Vicky would not have been able to have made herself heard or felt.

Later, when reflecting on Vicky's work with mentally and physically handicapped children, I realized how appropriate that was, for she herself had been in a handicapped condition during those two years so would be able to identify, and be alongside, those who could not express themselves in the usual way.

75

Fact is sometimes stranger than fiction, isn't it? But, also, we can be blind to those 'coincidences' and connections that weave their way through our lives like gossamer threads. If we could become more aware of the 'livingness' within creation our perception would be enlarged and less tunnel-visioned.

I eagerly await your thoughts on all this.

Lovingly,

U.

From Ray

April 1987

Dear Mrs Ivens,

Ursula has asked me to write to you while she gets over the operation, and I am happy to share with you the little involvement I had with Vicky during those two years.

The last time I saw her well was when she came to Edinburgh to see her mother. I saw her framed in the living room doorway and I had a feeling that she would not be with us much longer. It seemed crazy as she was in good health and in her prime. There was a sort of shadow about her. My practical, bossy 'self' told my discerning 'self' not to be stupid and I left it at that. We passed the time of day and I left.

The next time I saw her she was in hospital. Ursula had asked me if I would come and visit her, and if I could come in regularly, especially while she was away. I said that I would, although I was scared stiff at the prospect. On the mundane level the idea of trying to communicate with an inert body, the owner of which I hardly knew, filled me with dread. So I sent up a prayer and hoped that no one else would be there when I was and maybe I could muddle along: at least I knew Vicky couldn't rebuke me for my efforts.

Ursula and I went together the first time. Vicky was lying propped up, her face and body paralysed, but her large luminous eyes open. We did not know then that she was blind. Because I hadn't known her well, I couldn't remember how she used to look, so it was good to see photos of her on the bedside table: one was of her wearing green wellies at the edge of a river, fishing, and the other was with her children. Through these I could hold a 'well' picture of her in my mind. It was heartrending because I knew medically there was little hope of much recovery, yet I also knew that each case is very individual and that there are miracles. I had read recently of a man in Australia who had had a serious head injury and had been in a coma for a while, and who was now leading a normal life. Why not her?

I began to visit once or twice every two or three weeks. At first I would dread it and on my way to the hospital I would frantically think of things which I could say, and I would be so relieved if she was asleep and I could tiptoe away. Gradually I became used to the visits and grew to enjoy seeing her. I even wondered if I should speak to her about an experience I had as a young child so one day when she seemed fearful, I told her of a time when I had a high fever (I lived in Africa and had malaria) and how I experienced a wonderful feeling of endless space and warmth, light and peace, and how, just as I was beginning to merge my 'self' with it, I felt my 'self' drawn back into my earthly

77

body. I felt so cheated, despondent and annoyed at being deprived of this blissful state. I told her this to let her know that if it was death she was afraid of, she need not be. I hoped it would help.

On other days she would lie with her eyes focused at a far distance and in them there was an expression of wonder, joy and peace. On these days I would sit with her in great tranquillity and leave so full of happiness because of the living, vital presence in her room. Those were the days that she visited me! Was she then touching that place of light and warmth and peace?

It was good when I could talk about Ursula – what she was doing and when she would next come to visit. Her face would 'light up' in a real way so I knew she understood. When I came I would usually tell her about the day outside, describe the flowers in her room and give them to her to smell. Her room was always full of flowers whatever the season, because we knew that she loved them so much. I liked to sit beside her on the bed and hold her hand or touch her forehead. Best of all I liked reading poetry to her from *The Prophet*, which she liked, and latterly I read *Mr God, This is Anna* to her. She seemed to be listening and receiving some comfort.

There was a time a few weeks after the accident when I saw how distraught the immediate family were, and because I was less involved, I took it upon myself to talk to her about them. I said how devastated and upset they were, and how they longed for her to be well, but they did not want to prevent her going if it was 'right' for her. Deep down in themselves they wanted what was best for Vicky and would manage without her and come to terms with their sorrow.

78

All the time there were so many questions I wanted to ask her. Did she understand when we spoke? Did she know the people who came to visit? Did she want to speak? What did she feel? Did she know what had happened to her? Would it be better for her not to know than be aware and know that she might not ever be whole again? I would imagine her getting a little better so that she could go home and be cared for, but what of the frustrations, and how would it be after two years, five years, ten years? The doctors maintained that the brain was too badly damaged for Vicky to respond to events. But were they right? Those friends, family and nursing staff doubted it. Where was she in that still body? Where was the unique, 'you-ness' of Vicky? Sometimes I knew she was in her body in the bed and sometimes I sensed she was far away. Was she in that place and space where I had been twice in my life? Some people would call it another level of consciousness, others another dimension. It feels as if we are on the other side of our earthly life existence and can look down and glimpse the threads which link us to each other, and so can pass into death knowing that these links will never be broken in time or eternity. In this state, or inner place, the clamours and demands, the attachments of our earthly life no longer affect us. They are suddenly no longer important; we know we are passing and transient, yet our 'self' is not. We sense a love we never dreamed of as the foundation of our existence. Is this where Vicky was sometimes? Did she slip in and out of these levels, from her physical body to this other realm and perhaps sometimes toward the light of the world of the spirit?

How must it have been to be in a vehicle so wanting? One that could not see, nor speak, nor move, nor feed itself, one that needed everything done for it? How was it to be in such a body? When I was a child I had found it difficult enough finding my 'self' entombed in a normal, healthy body, and often during those two years I would wonder how it was for her. Sometimes I would come in and find that the radio had been left on a pop music programme and I would wonder how she could bear it, because I know that I would have hated it and been inwardly screaming to have it turned off! In fact I went home and told my children that if ever I was in a similar condition would they please ensure that this type of programme was never played! I don't like it very much at the best of times, let alone when I am not well.

So I searched for meaning in all this. I witnessed the struggle that was going on inside her, and at times it seemed like really hard work. Did she begin the backward journey through her life while she was lying there, which some Teachers tell us that we do after death? That would make sense. She brought us wisdom and joy as well as pain and despair. The hospital staff loved her.

These are some of the questions I would like answered but maybe they are irrelevant. Maybe they are only of interest in this world and not in the next.

When April comes and there are primroses in the secret places that only primroses know, and daffodils are in profusion on the banks and under the trees, I am always reminded of Vicky as her room at the hospital in springtime was always full of them, brought up from her garden at home.

Much later I went with Ursula to Vicky's graveside. I found this very healing. I seemed to feel her presence and that she was happy and free, released from the bondage of her body.

I hope some of Vicky's story may be of help to you in your grief for the loss of your husband.

With affectionate memories of you both and your hospitality on board 'Mallard',

Ray

December 1987

My dear,

What would I do without your receptive ear, receiving all that is taking place here, both on the spiritual level and on the physical level. It often seems that fact is stranger than fiction, and I don't always have words to describe what is happening – behind the actual 'happening', if you see what I mean!

I am very aware of Vicky helping me with the book I am writing at present. I also feel that parts are coming from a place in me with which I am not fully in touch. I daresay that some would call it our superconscious, or even our 'higher-self'. If only we could put our little self aside and consciously link up with this Self, allowing 'It' to live through us, then our lives and all we thought and did would be more fruitful and helpful to us and the world at large. Just occasionally, in spite of ourselves, the 'higher-self' does seem to be able to override our lower levels and then we really do go with the flow – the *wu-wei* as the Taoists say. Is that the same as doing God's will, I wonder? I think St Ignatius might have said it is 'Allowing God to be God in us'.

The other day I made a casual remark to Joyce to the effect that I must get a move on with the book, and instantaneously I was flooded with what I can only describe as electric-shock like vibrations which shot through my limbs to the ground. The unusual strength of the energy left me feeling quite weak at the knees. I suppose I was not able to absorb or integrate them with my own energies. There was nothing at all unpleasant or frightening about the experience, other than that it was a new one for me. I was left with no doubt that I would be helped with the writing, and that I had to get on with it. It was as simple as that. The tinglings always cease when I have made a note of the point. Vicky always did say what she wanted in a clear, precise, factual way, and these energies were conveying the same characteristics.

At times when I am writing a new line of thought will impress itself on my mind and I wonder how I am going to weave it into the current theme, so I pause for a break, go into another room, where I am led to a book I have not yet read, and there I find the answer. It was in this way I found *The Secret Life of Plants*, explaining how experiments have been carried out on plants which have been connected up to a kind of lie detector and monitoring has shown that they do pick up our thoughts and emotions. What a lot of unexplored areas there are as regards communication with other forms of life.

One hundred years ago we could not have believed it possible to communicate via air waves or radio frequencies, and today we find it difficult to entertain the thought that telescopic signals could come from beings in outer-space. At times when I am made aware of channels of communication yet to be recognised, it is as if I cannot get properly tuned in: the reception is fuzzy, similar to our television channels below number four. I suppose it stands to reason that these other air frequencies that surround us cannot come into use unless there is a receiver. In the same way electricity is in the ether but needs to be earthed and connected up to a circuit before it can be utilized; to effect a line of communication there has to be a transmitter and a receiver – a response to the other energy, for without that acknowledgement we only get a one-way transmission.

In my work I find many people are experiencing shifts of consciousness, but when this happens too suddenly it can cause much confusion, and we need someone who has been there before us to talk with and reassure us. When we can no longer hold on to lifelong beliefs, we may feel there is nothing left, and this can be scary, bewildering, even painful, until the fresh concept has been fully integrated. I am sure you find that there are compensations for having many years behind you? Hindsight helps to make us more philosophical when on a downward spiral, for we have learnt from experience that when we reach the bottom we shall turn and go upwards again – not that we are spared the pain, but it is less intense than in our youth. We also grow in wisdom as distinct from knowledge, and it is this wisdom that you share with me which I greatly value.

Thank you for that jewel of a sentence which says, 'I find that as one gets old one grows out of theology; all those sorts of questions fade, and terms like His, Him, He, only confine God to me now. Whatever God may be, it is far beyond the terms we use. One has seen this in theory, now one feels it in fact.'

Oh, yes, to feel it – to experience it – instead of

knowing it cerebrally is a big step along the path, and a great gift.

I am looking forward to being with you next week.
With my love,
U.

≫≷≸≪

Ascension Day, 12 May 1988

My dear,

Today I was led to look up Luke's description of the Ascension and two things struck me. First, how full of joy and peace the disciples were when their Master departed this earth-plane for the last time. That was exactly how I felt when sitting beside Vicky's hospital bed as she withdrew to the place that was awaiting her. On reflection, that was not an altogether usual reaction for a mother to have as her offspring left her physical body; especially as I had always been fearful of death scenes. My mother's funeral was the only one I had attended – and that was under protest. So the intense feeling of joy I felt, which stayed with me for six days, was quite out of character. Secondly, the reading helped me to perceive the Resurrection in a new light. It began to dawn on me that Christ's Ascension was showing us that one day we will all pass on in like manner; our present dense, physical energy patterns will be changed into a 'light' body that will vibrate at a higher frequency. We, too, will be able to pass through physical forms, walk on water and come and go once we have absorbed the Christ Consciousness – once we can live and experience the message Christ had for us all. The physicists, such as Fritjof Capra, who are exploring and monitoring the different energy patterns of various forms of matter, with their unique vibrations, help us to understand that death is but a moving into a higher, finer energy pattern.

After all, the caterpillar emerges from its chrysalis as a butterfly, and the cicada breaks free from the skin it has outgrown into new, transparent life. I guess what we have to do first and foremost is to get rid of the limited perception we have of who we are, as this keeps us encapsulated in a form that the evolutionary process is prompting us to shed.

Is it not becoming more obvious that communication between the 'two worlds' is a natural interpenetration and mingling of different energy levels? In reality there is but one 'world' for we all occupy the same space. There is no separation, it is we who create the division within our minds. The smell of damp, spring flowers which has come to me in mid-winter; the electric-like vibrations (for want of a better description) that have passed through me as I sensed Vicky's presence were more real than real at the time, and I knew without a shadow of a doubt that it was Vicky trying to communicate something. Yet later when I got sucked back into 'this world' thinking and into the nitty-gritty business of living, I would find myself doubting. . . . Why do we fall into this trap so often? It was the same after I made my thirty-day retreat. There would be times when I would doubt the reality of my experiences in meditation; although at the same time a part of me knew which was the Reality. There is still more integration of our higher and lower selves needed, I would say. Learning can be a slow process, can't it?

When I cast my mind back to the extract I read at

the Memorial Service, from the Abbé de Tourville's *Letters*, I knew the reality of being '. . . . in close and constant communion (with them); our life only separated from theirs by the thinnest of veils'. At the time I knew the truth of it at a level somewhere between the head and the heart. Today it is knowing beyond thinking and feeling – IT IS. Isn't this similar to what you wrote last December when you described how you felt about God today – remember? 'Whatever God may be, it is far beyond the terms we use. One has seen this in theory, now one knows it in fact.' Yes? IT IS. . . .

How is your own writing getting on? I do understand how maddening meal-time interruptions must be. Thought-threads get lost as well as vital pieces of paper which get tidied away! Keep going in spite of the setbacks, and know that you help me to continue to push the pen.

Love as always,

U.

~≈~

From Joyce

August 1988

Dear Mrs Ivens,

Although you do not know me, Ursula suggested I write to you because of your long connection with her family. I would like to relate some of the unexpected incidents which have taken place when she and I have been together.

I met Ursula just four years ago at a weekend workshop at the Cenacle, Grayshott. It was one of those rare occasions when you talk to someone for the first time and suddenly find you seem to have known them for years. A double rare for me, because I do not find it easy to talk to 'strangers' – yet there I was sharing my inmost dreams with someone I had just met, finding to my joy that in many ways we shared a similar hope and vision for the future.

In time Ursula told me about her family and I learned how her daughter, Vicky, had been very badly brain-damaged after a simple operation. She spoke of the hopes they had that perhaps she would recover enough to at least be able to go home, but admitted that the medical advice was against this. I learned of the trauma and anguish of the family as they struggled to come to terms with the situation and the ever present hope that perhaps the next visit would see the longed for improvement. Ursula was convinced that Vicky responded to her voice; that she was aware of her presence. On my first visit to Edinburgh I was privileged to visit the hospital and meet Vicky. As I sat by her bedside there was no doubt that she did respond to voices: mine causing more agitated movements, whereas there was an acceptance of Ursula's presence that was more easily felt than explained. It was just after a time when we had been sharing together the possibility of Vicky being moved from the hospital to home that Ursula rang to say that her condition had unexpectedly deteriorated. When she telephoned again to say that Vicky had died I could only join with her family in thankfulness that Vicky was free at last from that poor tormented body.

Since then Ursula and I have continued to meet from time to time to enjoy each other's company, to share experiences, books, dreams etc. It was at one such time, when Ursula was staying for a few days after Christmas, that Vicky first came. We had been sitting over our evening meal and Ursula had been talking about Vicky; how she had been as a child; what she had been like as an adult and her approach to life. She spoke about her own relationship to Vicky and how they had become so much closer as they shared and edited her previous book, *Christian Evolution*. That evening I really felt I was beginning to understand and know Vicky as a person rather than as Ursula's daughter. I also remember feeling that being able to talk about Vicky could be therapeutic for her. Having finished our meal we adjourned to the kitchen and I began to wash up. We were still talking when I had a most strange experience. My whole body was shaken by what I can only describe as an 'electric shock' and inside I could hear someone shouting so plainly 'My Mother', over and over again. Have you ever had that cold feeling where your hair seems to stand on end? If you have you will understand the feeling that swept through me. The voice inside was quite separate from my own inner chattering. There was such urgency in that calling, but I in no way wished to add to Ursula's grief by announcing that somehow I could hear Vicky so I lamely said: 'Something most odd is happening to me. Do you know I think Vicky is here with us.' I was therefore somewhat surprised when Ursula replied that she knew Vicky was there and had felt her presence for some time. Then my body once more was engulfed in this feeling of being shaken by a current: so strong I had to hold on to the sink. I went on to say to Ursula, 'She really is here, the feeling is very strong' but my voice was distorted and I could hear the voice inside shouting, 'Help me! Help me!'. It felt as if Vicky wanted to speak through me, if only I knew how. I was in tears because I could feel her need so deep inside and was upset because in some way I felt I had failed her, that I had not been able to reach her. The telephone rang at this point. As I picked it up my legs were still shaking, my voice still distorted and my thoughts completely incoherent. I am sure the person on the other end of the telephone must have thought I had been drinking.

I was completely confused by this experience. I had no idea what to make of it. To be honest 'contact with the spirits' was something I treated, not with disbelief, but certainly with great scepticism. I did have a phase of using a Ouija board and had come to the conclusion that some energy, possibly from the participants, moved the glass but I had to admit that I could feel when the energy left. I had also visited, on three occasions, the Spiritualist Centre in London on a 'fact-finding mission'. I had been surprised by the openness (no darkened rooms or hidden wires), just an ordinary lady standing and talking to the audience from a slightly raised platform. She did tell me things about my grandmother which my mother later corroborated, but the encounter did not inspire me to pursue the matter. I could not see the point of such contact (if contact there was) and had since given very little thought to such matters.

There was nothing within my own experience therefore that enabled me to rationalize what had happened. It was completely bizarre, things like that just do not happen in ordinary every-day kitchens! Being rather like an ostrich who puts his head in the sand when danger is about in the hope that it will go away, I found I did not want to think about what happened. I seemed unable to talk about it to Ursula and in fact she was aware of this and the whole incident was just dropped for that evening. Next day, we were standing talking in the hall when it happened again. This time both of us felt the waves of energy which, for me, have come to mean that Vicky is around. This time as a joint experience it was easier to talk about. It was almost as though Vicky was giving me verification through Ursula that the experience was a 'reality'. She *was* communicating. (I don't know why as human beings we find a greater surety in our own experience through the affirmation of others, but we do, and for me, it was a tremendous release.) So we then shared how we were feeling, what exactly had happened to each of us, and why we thought Vicky was communicating. I could feel her concern for Ursula and felt that in some way she was seeking our help.

Ursula was convinced that Vicky was not there because of her, but for something more urgent. I could feel that sense of urgency but also the concern. Ursula thought it might be something to do with the next book she was writing: this she had been discussing with her before the operation. As Ursula mentioned the book we were once again engulfed in that surge of energy and we knew that this was the reason for the communication. As I write this I wonder why we were so convinced. The only explanation I can give is that the affirmation was in the 'feel' of that energy surge: a positive rather than a negative impulse followed by a sense of enlightenment that dawns after a long struggle to gain an understanding or solution to a problem. So, we knew it was the book, but as Ursula said – 'Where to begin?' We should just have said 'Leave it to Vicky', it would have saved a great deal of turmoil for Ursula over the next few months, but our relationship with Vicky had only just begun.

Mostly she comes when Ursula and I are together; often agreeing or disagreeing with what is being worked through, communicating through the energy surge. When I was in Edinburgh lunching at the Art Gallery she came so strongly and was so insistent that I just had to mention her presence to Ursula, who was already aware that Vicky was with us but had not said anything to me about it. It would appear that Vicky's insistent 'nudging' comes when she wishes us both to acknowledge her presence. We were discussing our meeting with Annie and Maisie: into the conversation came Maisie's assertion that because of her serious handicap, Vicky had already been working for a long time out of her body. The intense feeling of emotion that flowed through me from Vicky at this point had me wiping my eyes, somewhat embarrassedly, as I sat at the table. It was such a deep, deep feeling that she so wanted us to understand how it had been for her not being able to communicate this awareness to those she loved. Another time when we were meditating together Janice was given the title of this book and a guideline to its form. Again I was able to feel her tremendous relief and delight that her message was getting through at last! When Janice, the next night, suggested we should seek verification, Vicky's exasperation burst through and I heard myself saying 'Oh come on, she told us plainly enough yesterday', in such an authoritarian voice, that the room went suddenly quiet – if you know what I mean! Vicky's concern for her mother is always strong but I was to see this extended when we visited her own home. I met her youngest son Fergus for the first time and suddenly found that I had an almost overwhelming desire to hug him. Again I could sense Vicky so close. Having a great respect for children it is not in my nature to go around inflicting my presence on them in such a manner; but this feeling to touch him became irresistible and in the end I just lightly touched the top of his head – and then there was peace.

I still cannot explain or rationalize what is happening. I do not see Vicky and rarely hear her. Our communication comes through waves of energy and emotions: this mode of contact has enabled me to accept the authenticity of what has happened as a 'reality' for me. To 'see' or 'hear' Vicky could be inner projections, but the spontaneous feelings of emotion which well up from somewhere in my solar plexus cannot be self-imagined. They arrive without warning, unexpectedly, and often when I have no idea Vicky is present.

So through Vicky I have learned that communication is possible and that channels can be opened: in fact many people are now saying that the 'veil' between the two worlds is getting thinner. But for what reason? Not just to keep in touch with families and loved ones, however important this may be. There seems to be a sense of urgency that comes through again and again, so insistent that it cannot be ignored. In fact the urgency has been so great that at times I have found it quite frightening. Brother Roger wrote: 'Perhaps this sense of urgency springs from an awareness of living on borrowed time, with the past on the verge of destruction and perhaps a whole civilization with it.' Yet the polarity of this is the glimmering of an understanding of what the New Age has in store: *koinonia* – reciprocal love – God in, with and working through us. No longer the loneliness of separation but the 'uniqueness of each individual person within a community of belonging together' – each giving and receiving, enriching and at the same time being enriched by, the Whole. The purpose of Vicky's communication seems to be to urge us on towards this new understanding.

I do hope you will not mind my writing, but personally it has helped enormously to put these unusual experiences into words and to look at them objectively. There are so few people I could talk to about such things without being considered odd, dealing with the occult or dabbling in Spiritualism. I just do not believe that any of these labels apply to myself or to the happenings I have related to you. Yet I cannot deny the reality of these experiences even though I admit it is a reality of which I was previously unaware. I feel that Vicky has opened my own inner awareness and that in some way I now have a responsibility to share this understanding with others. Do you not agree?

Thank you so much for being a listening ear.

Yours sincerely,

Joyce

From Mary

September 1988

Dearest Ursula,

You asked me to put on paper for you my recollections of the gossamer threads of coincidence that have connected me, through you, with Vicky's tragedy. I did not know Vicky as well as your other children, but because I always heard so much about her, I felt closer to her than our actual meetings warranted. Here then, for what they are worth, are my thoughts and memories of those events, and also the copy of 'James's Song' which you asked for. This has now been set to music by a young musician from Leeds, and we hope to use it somehow to benefit handicapped children.

Do you remember the large marble clock in our kitchen? It has been there for years, but I was surprised when someone commented on its beautiful chime, because I was unaware that it had one! In fact it strikes not only the hours, but the quarters as well, and it seems unbelievable that I could have spent so much time in the same room as the clock and not have heard it. Now that it has been pointed out to me, I *always* hear it strike: I have become aware of it.

I have looked up the word 'coincidence' in several dictionaries. Some define it as a 'chance occurrence at the same time or place', but one describes it as a 'simultaneous happening with no *apparent* cause'. It is this word, apparent, that I think is important.

A year after Vicky's accident, you and I were together on Iona at a conference, and naturally she was much in our minds. We discussed endlessly the possibility that, despite medical opinion, Vicky might have some awareness of what was going on around her, and being said to her. You were keen that I should see her, and I agreed, with some trepidation, to visit her with you on my way home from Scotland. I knew that you would be watching my face to see what my reaction was, and felt afraid lest I should either give you false hope, or cast you deeper into despair, and I felt very inadequate. As it turned out we were unable to go to the hospital at the same time, and I went on my own.

As you know I've always been hopeless at following

directions, and did not know my way round Edinburgh, so I was worried in case I got lost or couldn't park. It seems a shaming admission in the face of such dreadful trauma that I should have been fussing about such trivia, but it was a relief when I reached the Infirmary, an imposing Victorian building, and drove into the small forecourt in which I remember flowering cherry trees and 'No Parking' signs. I left the engine running, anxious not to waste the limited time available, and nipped up the steps to enquire from Reception what I should do. No Reception desk! No people at all! Clearly I was in the wrong place, and I thought of the two hundred miles I had to drive home, with a time deadline. At that moment a group of nurses appeared. I asked the way to Ward 25, and enquired where I could park. They told me that I was in the wrong building altogether and would have to drive round a complicated one-way system to get to the right entrance, several streets away, when one nurse, a pretty fair-haired girl, suddenly asked: 'Are you going to see Vicky Maclay?' I said I was. She said there was a way through from this old building to the other part of the hospital, but that I would be sure to get lost and that she would take me there. She added (despite signs to the contrary!) that my car would be alright, so I turned off the engine and followed her through a complicated network of corridors to another building. I asked her how on earth she had guessed that I was going to see Vicky, assuming, wrongly, that Ward 25 must be a very small ward. She said that she had just had 'a funny feeling'. She had only worked on that ward for a few weeks during her training some nine months previously, but remembered Vicky vividly, though she had not seen her since. I thanked her warmly and told her she was an angel!

It was only later that it dawned on me what an extraordinary 'apparent' coincidence this was, the odds must have been very much against it in such a huge hospital, especially as I had not even mentioned that I was visiting anyone, but merely asked directions. I am sure of this.

My half hour with Vicky remains a vital and moving memory for which I am grateful. There was, of course, no physical response, but I had a deep feeling of communication. I would not have cared to say anything in that room that I would not have wished her to hear, no matter how impossible this was supposed to be. I felt relieved to be alone with her, and therefore unselfconscious, but I also remember feeling privileged and humble. I told her how beautiful she still was, no matter how wracked and distorted her body might be, but above all I remember saying over and over again the words of Julian of Norwich: 'All shall be well, and all shall be well, and all manner of things shall be well.'

There was no parking ticket on my car, and I had a wonderfully easy run home to Yorkshire.

A year later, I was again on Iona in May, though just about to leave, when you arrived for a retreat, and the news came through that Vicky had done a 'nose-dive' and was failing. Together with others, I joined you in the Oran chapel at about 10 p.m. to pray for her. I remember visualizing her spirit as a bird taking wing and hearing the wild crying of a seagull. Four days later Vicky died. You were due to come and stay with me on 30th May on your way to St Beuno's, and as it turned out you came immediately after Vicky's funeral.

Last summer, another year later and again just after a week on Iona, I was busy planting dahlias for our autumn border when the words of a song arrived, fully fledged, in my head: a song for James, our handicapped grandson, then aged three. It is very simple, perhaps even a cliché, and not a poem I would normally consider sending for publication. Nevertheless it came into my head like instant dictation and I have been told that it in some way 'speaks' to quite a few people who have dealings with handicapped children. I rushed indoors and wrote the verses down on the back of an envelope. Most poems come with hard work and wrestling; if a poem does 'arrive', it only comes partially, and I have to work to match the 'received' bit, and always I nit-pick and revise, but James's song arrived complete, and I have never altered a word. I remember thinking of Vicky as I wrote it down: of her locked body and 'baffled eyes'.

You had not been in touch for some time, so when you telephoned me that same day to tell me that you believed you knew that Vicky's work now is to do with mentally handicapped children, I felt as if I had been given an electric shock.

Some people might say that this is all very tenuous, that the gossamer thread which connects these small incidents is of no significance, and they might of course be right, but the clock goes on striking whether we hear the chimes or not and I think it behoves us to listen.

Here are my memories for you, sent with much love. James is making remarkable progress.

Mary

James's Song

Oh did you volunteer to come
And how long will you stay
And can we learn enough of love
Before you slip away?

We greeted you with fear and grief
You seemed beyond our reach
But now we know a child of light
Who has so much to teach.

Sometimes you look through baffled eyes
Which fills our hearts with pain.
Oh is it that we are obtuse
And you cannot explain?

We march our roads with hustled tread
You step a different pace
But your path may be more direct
To reach your special place.

Oh did you volunteer to come
And how long will you stay
To teach us unconditional love
Before you go away?

Mary Sheepshanks

EPILOGUE

CHANGING OUR CONSCIOUSNESS

We read the world wrong and say that it deceives us.
                    Rabindranath Tagore, *Stray Birds* LXXV

I believe that the related experiences of those involved
with Vicky over the two years of her hospitalization
and subsequent death, bring us to the edge of a new
understanding of communication which is available to
everyone. There are many people in the world who
having reached that edge, have moved beyond it and
are firmly established within this wider realm; but there
are many more who are still standing on the periphery,
often fearful to take the next step. We need to help each
other to understand that there is no need to be afraid of
stepping into the unknown. Fear and love (acceptance)
cannot inhabit the same space; when fear takes over
there can be no growth.

Little by little we realize that we are all invisibly
connected by gossamer threads which are used and
woven into the tapestry of the Plan. Our finite minds
cannot grasp the connections, or the reasons behind so
many of life's incidents. We are only beginning to be
aware that there can be no such thing as separation from
each other, or from the One. Each can help or hinder

101

our pilgrimage, affecting one another as we dance through the one space.

We find ourselves at a crisis point in the history of the world, but it is also a time of opportunity. This transitional period gives us the opportunity to take a leap in our understanding and move forward to the next spiral on the evolutionary plan. This wider vision is often called Cosmic Consciousness, or the Christ Consciousness. New and improved technology and scientific progress will not aid the evolutionary process unless there is this change of consciousness.

This change of heart and mind will not come out of old thought patterns and concepts which we have outgrown; nor will the change be found in the present dimension, in which we are in danger of being held. This is not to say that past concepts have been wrong, for they brought us to the point we are at today. But now is the time for us to grow up and question the validity of the tramlines along which our conditioned minds still travel, and allow our ways of perceiving to change. This means querying much of what we have taken for granted through our lack of awareness and tunnel vision.

We are not the same person we were yesterday; our very cells have died off and been replaced by new ones. The experiences we interact with daily change our thoughts and feelings, as did Vicky's death for me. They can add to our stature or detract from it, depending upon our reaction to these circumstances. Creation is about growth and we can no longer think like children, or stay in an adolescent stage, in spite of the lure of security and carefreeness that these stages may suggest. We, unlike other forms of life, have the ability to choose; we can say yes or no to change as our will determines. The time has come to wake up, stop being sleep walkers, and become aware of who we are and where we are going, and how we are being called to co-operate in the evolving of creation. The decisions and choices in life are ours and we now have to take responsibility for our lives, which means acting more consciously rather than reacting out of past habits. We need the extra perception that the consciousness of those who have gone beyond the veil can impart. Our work is to discern what is given, or channelled, and if it rings true to us, to follow that Way. No one is right or wrong and our response to the Call will vary in its uniqueness.

Yet as well as learning to focus outwards we need also to look inwards. Eastern spirituality tells us that our Guru is within, and Carl Jung and psychoanalysts who have followed him have shown us that there is another whole dimension waiting to be uncovered and explored. Our journey has also to be an inward one, and each will be unique, for the God you may discover will not be the same as my God, and yet will be the same God who gives life to the Universe, and whose laws we must now recognize for the good of the Whole. This journey will take a lifetime – or as long as it takes – but we will be richly rewarded when we learn to trust our innermost thoughts and feelings. It was Jung's belief that there are no longer any new frontiers to explore except in the area of the psyche, the soul and the mind: that is where the hidden treasure lies – deep within each one of us.

There is recognition of the thinning of the veil between the two worlds, put so well by Richard Alpert (Ram Dass): 'It is like the moment depicted on the ceiling of the Sistine Chapel where the hands of God and man are just about to touch; it is at that moment when despair is at its greatest, when you reach up, that the Grace descends and you experience the knowledge/ intuition that it all is not, in fact, the way you thought it was.'

We hear a voice within telling us that things are not as they should be; the more we listen, the more we shall hear, for all knowledge is within and unfolds as we seek. So we, for our part, have to learn to listen with the inner-ear, a form of communication that is not always easy for us, and be open to a new perspective on both this world and the next. Two conditions are asked of us: we need to put aside time, to find space within which we can enter the Greater Silence; and we need to want, truly want, to find God. It is these times of meditation that help bring about the transformation and change in our consciousness that is asked of us today. Now is the time to wake-up and respond to the Call to become co-creators in building the New Jerusalem.

TRANSFORMATION

This book is a chapter out of one person's lifetime, yet in a sense it is our chapter, our lifetime – everyone's story, for we all share a common humanity. Within this shared humanity we can be in touch with feelings and thoughts that are to be found in the depths of our common being. So, my thoughts can be your thoughts, and your feelings can be experienced by me, the only difference is that they are brought forth from a different life-situation. We each have our own personal and unique way of responding to events, partially deter-mined by our upbringing, the conditioning imposed upon us by the home and society and our culture and education. Out of this disparity of lifestyles similar feelings are evoked and this enables us to share one another's joys and sorrows and fears in a very real way because, in varying degrees of intensity, we have been there too, or will likely be before the end of our pilgrimage on earth. It is comforting and strengthening to know that we are not alone in the variegated moods that weave their way through our life-pattern; and when we hit a low and find ourselves in extreme desolation we can think of others who have also been in the trough of despair and who have been carried through and out of it. This helps us to ride the storm without sinking, and in time we are able to be thankful for the opportunity to learn through the pain of it. Our reaction to adversity may help others to see that 'the facts are kind and God is in the facts'.

This common pool of feelings may be a part of what Jung termed the collective unconscious. If we can transform our feelings and adversities by working on our own reactions to the givens in life, and not allow ourselves to get carried away and sucked into life's melodramas, then we establish a peacefulness that will remain and be available, in the collective unconscious, for others to tap into when their need arises. Now is the time when our emotions, or the emotional body, is being cleansed. Sometimes our personal suffering and cleansing is not always to transform our own energies but can be used to heal other's emotions. The fire that purifies must eventually touch everyone. In the end this Fire, the Energy of Love, will transform the whole, as our evolutionary journey takes us toward Omega Point.

Every thought leaves its mark on the ether, which can be picked up by someone, at sometime. The more aware and sensitive we become the more this will happen. We have an enormous responsibility for our thoughts, if we did but realize, so let us be aware – beware – of our thoughts and make sure they are as positive as we are capable of making them; this is one way of helping to restore peace to the world.

Ian Fearn puts it well.

> All creation begins in thought. To make the new world we desire needs vision that begets new thinking, transcending familiar inclinations. Only as we unite to create a new thought-sphere can this new world come into being.

THE KEY

Nowadays an increasing number of people are making space for an hour or so in which to meditate silently together. This is replacing a chat over a cup of coffee – or the coffee takes second place! What is discovered is that the level of communication is greater and more profound in the silence than when there is a smoke-screen of words coming between what we are trying to convey of 'other world' experiences and the reality of this present level. Words can be a veritable stumbling block when trying to communicate a felt-experience that belongs to another dimension. In the silence we discover what it is we truly seek and, once we are in touch with the God-part of ourselves, we find our will or desire is not different from what we call God's will, for what seemed to be two opposing wills is in reality one and the same. When we have found the God within and experienced the peace and wisdom that is not of

106

'this world' – when that becomes a felt-knowledge, it becomes a part of us which we cannot lose; there can be no turning back for we know with an inner-knowing that surpasses belief. We all have spells when we feel out of step with the values of this world, when we do not seem to be able to blend this inner-knowing with the way things operate in daily life. In a moment of despair we vow we'll forget it all, and not bother our heads with these inner thoughts and feelings. But when it comes to the crunch we cannot do this. We have touched and tasted and are held by Something greater than ourselves. There is no turning back. Meditation is the gateway to these realms and, I believe, the key to the future unfolding of our spiritual evolution. It is during meditation, when we open ourselves to a Mind larger than our small minds, that a process of transformation is able to take place. We adopt the attitude of a flower that turns its petals to the sun, seeking life-giving energies to shine upon it. When we surrender and let go this brings about an inner freedom and liberation hitherto unknown. When we are able to be in touch with the power of God's Love and compassion we shall have found the key that can unlock the Energy which can transform the world. We are then able to have compassion for our own predicament which enables us to flow out with love and compassion to others working through their problems.

Albert Nolan, in *Jesus Before Christianity* wrote: 'God has now revealed himself as the God of compassion. Man's compassion for man releases God's power in the world, the only power that can bring about the miracles of the Kingdom' (p 84). Teilhard de Chardin wrote: 'Some day, after we have mastered the winds, the waves, the tides and gravity, we shall harness

107

for God the energies of love. Then for the second time in the history of the world, man will have discovered fire.'

I do not believe we ourselves can do anything, for it is more a matter of becoming. We have to become pure unconditional Love and Compassion, and that takes us along a narrow, stony path through the market place, where much purification of the ego or the self takes place. Today you can find this going on all around; the traumas and trials of suffering in life are now on an increased and enlarged scale. These fiery experiences have to be gone through if man's consciousness is to be transformed. Within the singeing and the burning of our 'stash', purification is taking place which later can be seen as a deep, inner healing. We have to remember that the fire cannot burn our essential Self, for we are a part of that Fire; it only burns away that to which we cling. The reason we experience pain or suffering is because we are clinging to something that is other than the fire, be it person, material possession or an idea of the image we may have of ourselves. We make the pain worse than it need be by holding on to our attachments and wishing to remain safe and secure in our lives.

Resistance always causes unnecessary pain. On the physical level if we tighten muscles instead of relaxing and going with the pain, if we fight against the migraine or do not allow ourselves to flow with whatever it is that is taking place, we make the pain more acute. When we can be the beholder and watch the body going through these different sensations without fighting against them we do not identify with the pain in the same way; it does not have the same power over us. My leg can hurt, but I am more than just my leg! In the same vein we forget that we are not the Do-er; we do because we are given the Life Force that breathes and lives through us, but we are not the cause.

We need each other's support and understanding on this journey as we also grow through an interaction of ideas and exchange of energies. So we write our stories to encourage the innumerable others, who feel and struggle like ourselves, within this process of transformation, on our Way to the freedom of a fuller life in the Whole.

POSTSCRIPT: MYSTERY
WITHIN THE PROCESS

Vicky undertook the first editing of *Christian Evolution: Moving Towards a Global Spirituality*, and there is no doubt that she played a large part in the writing of this book. She made her presence felt in so many ways peculiar to Vicky. She is persistent and insistent and communicates what is needed in her characteristically pointed, economical way, and she does not give up easily despite the poor reception this end.

The message we need to grasp more deeply is that there is a continuing form of life; a continuity of consciousness that actively serves the Whole. Our work does not end when we leave the physical body.

I have felt the presence of many souls behind Vicky, encouraging her as she is encouraging us, and I thank her for her perseverance, and for strengthening my own faith in God, as well as helping me to believe in myself; believe in what I know to be true, deep down, but do not always have the courage to affirm and live.

I would like to make a connection with the Epilogue in *Christian Evolution*, where I was stumbling towards a feeling that the island of Iona had a unique part to play in raising consciousness in the world. The veil separating other dimensions appears to be becoming looser. The physicists are deepening the concept of oneness, making sense to the intellect as well as the feelings, for they tell us that we, and all life, are basically an energy, and that all energies interact with one another as they occupy the same space. There truly are no divisions or hard and fast boundaries, for all life is one Great Whole. Teilhard de Chardin, the prophet, priest and scientist, sensed this and wrote in his letters to the Abbé Breuil. 'We must break through and go beyond appearances; never perhaps more than now, has the veil seemed to me so "without seam". . . .' It is one thing to say this and another to experience it. The rarified atmosphere on Iona makes it possible to spiral in and out of different dimensions, to come and go; to have a foretaste of how it will be in what we time-bound mortals call the 'future', and to experience episodes that belong to the 'past'.

It was on Iona that this book was compiled, and I believe that Vicky was able to help because of the thinness of the veil between 'this world and the next'. We are the bridge builders of the New World, and perhaps we should remember St Columba's prophecy: 'In Iona God will be born anew.' This time may it be in the hearts and minds of all who visit that Sacred Isle.